PEARSON
my World
Social Studies®

We Are Connected

PEARSON

Boston, Massachusetts
Chandler, Arizona
Glenview, Illinois
New York, New York

ISBN-13: 978-0-328-63939-7
ISBN-10: 0-328-63939-7
18 18

Program Consulting Authors

The Colonial Williamsburg Foundation
Williamsburg, Virginia

Dr. Linda Bennett
Associate Professor, Department of Learning, Teaching, & Curriculum
College of Education
University of Missouri
Columbia, Missouri

Dr. Jim Cummins
Professor of Curriculum, Teaching, and Learning
Ontario Institute for Studies in Education
University of Toronto
Toronto, Ontario

Dr. James B. Kracht
Byrne Chair for Student Success
Executive Associate Dean
College of Education and Human Development
Texas A&M University
College Station, Texas

Dr. Alfred Tatum
Associate Professor, Director of the UIC Reading Clinic
Literacy, Language, and Culture Program
University of Illinois at Chicago
Chicago, Illinois

Dr. William E. White
Vice President for Productions, Publications, and Learning Ventures
The Colonial Williamsburg Foundation
Williamsburg, Virginia

Consultants and Reviewers

PROGRAM CONSULTANT

Dr. Grant Wiggins
Coauthor, *Understanding by Design*

ACADEMIC REVIEWERS

Bob Sandman
Adjunct Assistant Professor of Business and Economics
Wilmington College–Cincinnati Branches
Blue Ash, OH

Jeanette Menendez
Reading Coach
Doral Academy Elementary
Miami, FL

Kathy T. Glass
Author, *Lesson Design for Differentiated Instruction*
President, Glass Educational Consulting
Woodside, CA

Roberta Logan
African Studies Specialist
Retired, Boston Public Schools/ Mission Hill School
Boston, MA

PROGRAM TEACHER REVIEWERS

Glenda Alford-Atkins
Eglin Elementary School
Eglin AFB, FL

Andrea Baerwald
Boise, ID

Ernest Andrew Brewer
Assistant Professor
Florida Atlantic University
Jupiter, FL

Riley D. Browning
Gilbert Middle School
Gilbert, WV

Charity L. Carr
Stroudsburg Area School District
Stroudsburg, PA

Jane M. Davis
Marion County Public Schools
Ocala, FL

Stacy Ann Figueroa, M.B.A.
Wyndham Lakes Elementary
Orlando, FL

LaBrenica Harris
John Herbert Phillips Academy
Birmingham, AL

Marianne Mack
Union Ridge Elementary
Ridgefield, WA

Emily Manigault
Richland School District #2
Columbia, SC

Marybeth A. McGuire
Warwick School Department
Warwick, RI

Laura Pula
Holmes Elementary
Chicago, IL

Jennifer Palmer
Shady Hills Elementary
Spring Hill, FL

Diana E. Rizo
Miami-Dade County Public Schools/Miami Dade College
Miami, FL

Kyle Roach
Amherst Elementary, Knox County Schools
Knoxville, TN

Eretta Rose
MacMillan Elementary School
Montgomery, AL

Nancy Thornblad
Millard Public Schools
Omaha, NE

Jennifer Transue
Siegfried Elementary
Northampton, PA

Megan Zavernik
Howard-Suamico School District
Green Bay, WI

Dennise G. Zobel
Pittsford Schools–Allen Creek
Rochester, NY

iii

Social Studies Handbook

⊙ Reading and Writing

Our Communities

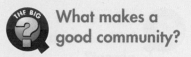

What makes a
good community?

A suburban street

Our Environment

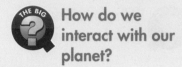

How do we interact with our planet?

Jack rabbit

Communities Build a Nation

THE BIG ? How does our past affect our present?

An early American flag

U.S. Government

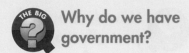 Why do we have government?

Mount Rushmore

Citizenship

How can I participate?

People helping others in their community

ix

A Growing Nation

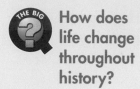

How does life change throughout history?

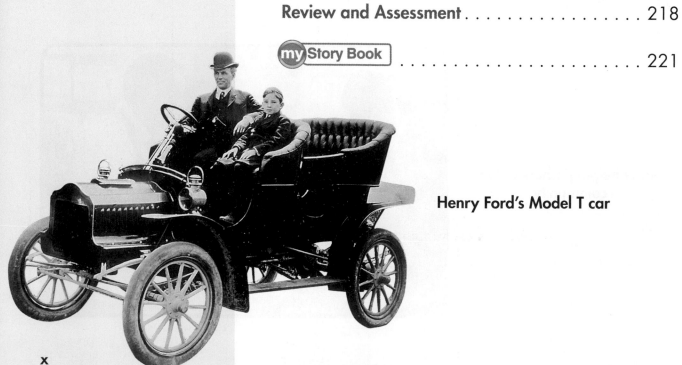

Henry Ford's Model T car

Working in Our Communities

THE BIG ? How do people get what they need?

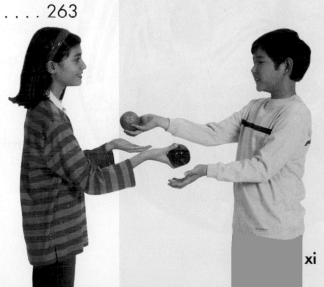

Friends exchanging fruit

Celebrating Our Communities

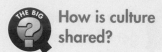

How is culture shared?

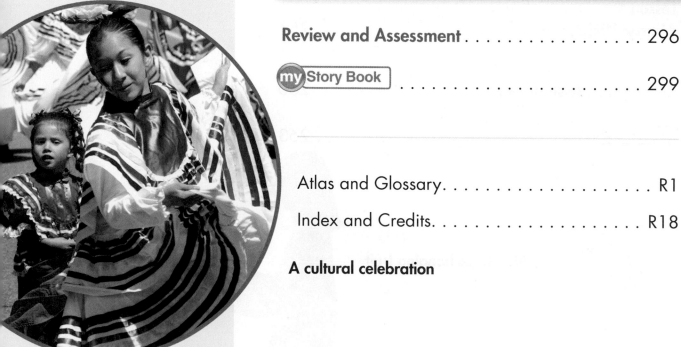

A cultural celebration

Reading Skills

Generalize

1

Cause and Effect

Cause

An effect is something that happens. A cause is why that thing happens.

As you read, ask yourself: What happened? Why did it happen?

Effect

Sequence

Sequence is the order of events.

First

Next

Last

Summarize

We summarize, or retell, to check our understanding of what we have read. A summary is short. It is no more than a few sentences.

Explorers travel to new lands. European explorers looked for a water route to the Americas.

Early Explorers

Fact and Opinion

A statement of fact can be proven true or false.
A statement of opinion tells someone's ideas or feelings.

Draw Conclusions

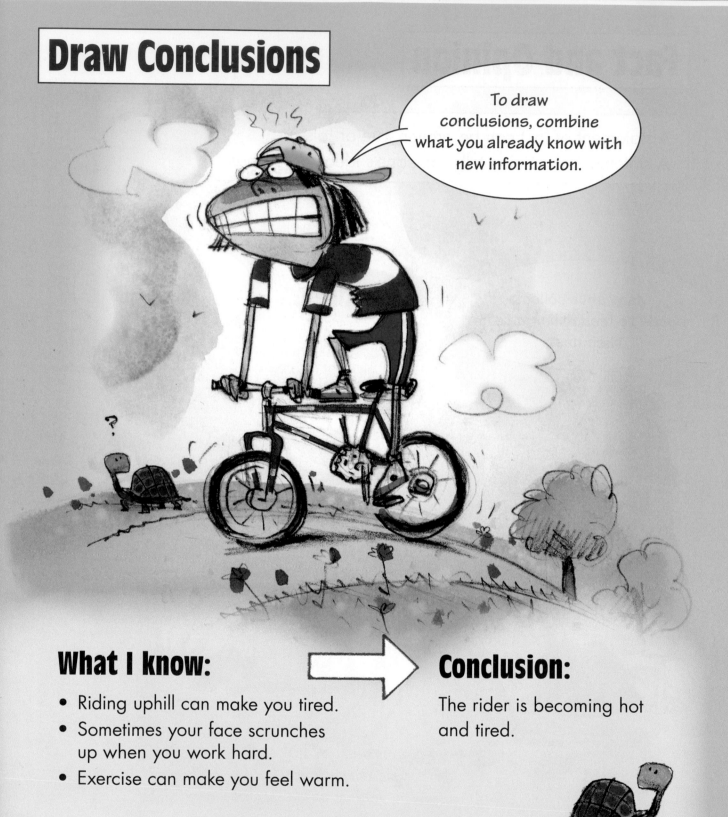

What I know:

- Riding uphill can make you tired.
- Sometimes your face scrunches up when you work hard.
- Exercise can make you feel warm.

Conclusion:

The rider is becoming hot and tired.

Reading Skills

Compare and Contrast

Alike	Different

8

Keys to Good Writing

The Writing Process

Good writers follow steps when they write. Here are five steps that will help you become a good writer!

Prewrite
- Choose a topic that you like.
- Gather details about your topic.

Draft
- Get all your ideas down on paper.
- Don't worry about making it perfect.

Revise
- Review your writing and share it with a friend.
- Look for the traits of good writing.
- Change parts that are unclear or incomplete.

Edit
- Check your spelling, capitalization, and punctuation.
- Make a final copy.

Share
- Share your writing with others.

The Writing Traits

Good writers look at six qualities of
their writing to make it the best work
possible.

Ideas

Ideas are your thoughts and
the message you want to share.
Choose ideas that are interesting
to you.

Organization

Organization means you put your thoughts in order.
Make your writing and your ideas easy to follow.

Voice

Voice means your writing sounds natural.
Write as if you were telling someone your story.

Word Choice

Word choice means you choose your
words carefully.
Make a clear picture for your readers.

Sentence Flow

Sentence flow means your writing is easy to read.
Use sentences of different lengths and with
different beginnings.

Conventions

Conventions are the rules of writing, such as
spelling, capitalization, and punctuation.
Correct any errors you find.

21st Century Learning
Online Tutor

You can go online to myworldsocialstudies.com to practice the skills listed below.
These are skills that will be important to you throughout your life.
After you complete each skill tutorial online, check it off here in your worktext.

⊙ Target Reading Skills

☐ Main Idea and Details   ☐ Generalize

☐ Cause and Effect   ☐ Compare and Contrast

☐ Classify and Categorize   ☐ Sequence

☐ Fact and Opinion   ☐ Summarize

☐ Draw Conclusions

Collaboration and Creativity Skills

☐ Solve Problems   ☐ Resolve Conflict

☐ Work in Cooperative Teams   ☐ Generate New Ideas

Graph Skills

☐ Interpret Graphs   ☐ Interpret Timelines

☐ Create Charts

Map Skills

☐ Use Longitude and Latitude   ☐ Interpret Economic Data on Maps

☐ Interpret Physical Maps   ☐ Interpret Cultural Data on Maps

Critical Thinking Skills

☐ Compare Viewpoints   ☐ Make Decisions

☐ Use Primary and Secondary Sources   ☐ Predict Consequences

☐ Identify Bias

Media and Technology Skills

☐ Conduct Research   ☐ Evaluate Media Content

☐ Use the Internet Safely   ☐ Deliver an Effective Presentation

☐ Analyze Images

Our Communities

 my Story Spark

What makes a good community?

Think about your community. Then **write** about people and places you see around you and what you do on a typical day in your community.

....

....

....

....

Arizona Communities

Exploring Nearby Communities

"I guess I live in a suburban neighborhood!" says Casey. "I never really thought about the difference." Casey lives in Arizona. He has been learning a lot in school about different types of communities. Some are urban communities, or in large cities. Then there are suburban communities, or smaller towns that are located near large cities. Farther away in the countryside where there is a lot of open space, there are rural communities. Now that Casey has learned about all of these communities, he wants to see for himself what they are like.

The first stop on Casey's community tour of Arizona is an urban community. Casey loves the downtown area. "There's always something to do," he says as he walks downtown with his mother. Casey looks around and sees people shopping, going to work, visiting museums, and walking their dogs. There are so many tall buildings. It seems like there are buses, cars, taxis, and trains everywhere!

Casey visited three different types of communities in Arizona.

Casey enjoys looking at all of the tall buildings.

Suburban communities, like Chandler, Arizona, have many houses with yards and driveways.

Casey climbs on the playground equipment in Chandler, Arizona.

More than 1 million people live in this urban community. Casey understands why so many people enjoy living in the city. Everything is so close! There are also many ways to have fun. "When it's hot, I can cool off in the city fountains!"

The next stop on Casey's tour is Chandler, a suburb that is also his hometown. Chandler is very close to the city. It is only about 25 miles away. Almost 250,000 people live in Chandler. Many people like living there because it is very easy to travel into the city. There are nearby highways that lead right into the city, or people can take a bus or train. "When we go downtown, it doesn't take very long," Casey says, walking around his suburban neighborhood. "But staying close to home is fun, too."

The streets of Chandler are much different from the streets in the city. The buildings are not as close together, and there are not a lot of crowds. Only a few people are crossing the street. Some people are walking in and out of the small shops. Casey then notices some children riding their bicycles toward a park. As Casey and his mother walk toward the playground, he sees a family playing with their dog in their front yard. There is definitely a lot more space here to run around!

14

Some rural communities have farms with many animals, like horses.

Casey and his grandpa like taking walks around the farm.

The final stop on Casey's tour is a rural community. This community is in the countryside, where towns are very small. Fewer than 1,500 people live there. Many people live and work on farms. People in cities and suburbs depend on these farms for fresh fruits and vegetables. "My grandpa lives in a rural community," says Casey. "He has the best peaches I've ever tasted! And lots of horses I can pet."

Casey and his grandpa take a walk toward the horses. As he sees the horses in the distance, Casey is amazed by all of the open space. Many people enjoy living here because there is so much peace and quiet. "I have more elbow room," says Casey's grandpa. "I like to relax and slow down out here." But his grandpa does enjoy visiting the suburbs or the city every now and then, too.

So, which community does Casey like best? "I liked touring all of these communities." says Casey. "They all have something special. They all have what it takes to make a good community!"

Think About It Based on this story, do you think you would like to live in a community different from your own? As you read the chapter ahead, think about what makes your community special.

Casey always enjoys petting the horses on his grandpa's farm.

Lesson 1

What Makes a Community?

Envision It!

These are pictures of the same community. Think about which picture is from the past and which is from the present.

Communities near Lake Michigan have water resources for fishing.

Where do you live? That's easy! You live in a community. A **community** is a place where people live, work, and have fun together. Communities are alike in many ways. People in communities help each other. They care about the safety of their communities. They follow laws, or rules, to make their communities safe places to live, work, and play. Many people have jobs or businesses. For fun, people join clubs and sports teams, go shopping, and see movies.

Settling in a Community

People settle in communities based on **location**, or where something needed can be found. Communities need good natural resources, such as water, soil, and trees. A **natural resource** is something found in nature that is useful to people. People might choose to settle in a community where there are water resources, such as lakes and rivers. For example, a community near a body of water would be a good place to settle for people who enjoy fishing or work in the fishing industry. People can also use water resources for traveling.

16

UNLOCK THE BIG ?

I will know ways in which communities are the same and different.

Vocabulary

community   mineral

location   diverse

natural   culture
  resource

region

Label the picture from the past with a 1. Label the picture from the present with a 2.

Other people might choose to settle in a community where there are land resources, such as good soil. If a community has rich soil, farmers can live and work there. Others might choose to settle there because they can get fresh fruits and vegetables from farmers. People can like different things about the same community.

Trees are also an important land resource. If a community has a lot of trees, people can use the trees for building homes, schools, and stores. They can keep building so that the community grows.

1. **⊙ Main Idea and Details Fill in** the chart with two more details to support the main idea.

People settle in communities where there are good natural resources.

Farmers can work in communities that have good soil.

Communities in Regions

Communities have been settled in all 50 states of the United States. Some states are located in the North, the South, the East, or the West. Some states are in the middle of our country, too! Different groups of states are located in different regions. A **region** is an area with common features that set it apart from other places.

Some states are located in regions where there are many mountains. The Rocky Mountains are some of the highest in the United States. People like to settle near the mountains because of some of the activities they can enjoy there. They can ski and sled in winter. In summer, they can go camping, hiking or mountain climbing.

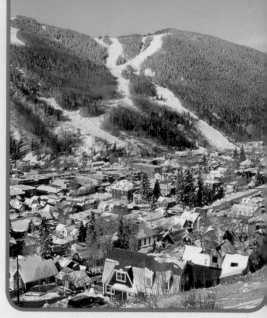

A community in the mountains

Beach communities can be found in some regions along the shoreline, near the coasts. Some people settle there because they enjoy swimming or surfing. Others settle near the shoreline because of jobs they can do there. People can work in restaurants that serve the seafood from the ocean.

Some regions have communities located near mineral resources such as coal or iron. A **mineral** is a resource that does not come from an animal or a plant. Businesses that produce items made with minerals are located in these communities.

A community near a beach

18

People in Communities

People from all over the world form communities. Many people in communities have jobs. Some people work as doctors, teachers, car mechanics, police officers, or mail carriers. When people are not working, they enjoy different activities. People might participate in their favorite activities, such as gardening, riding bicycles, or playing a sport. Others might try new activities they have never done before.

Many communities have **diverse**, or different, cultures. **Culture** is the way of life of a group of people. Some communities hold festivals, parades, and fairs to honor these cultures. Sedona, Arizona, is proud of its diverse community. Sedona celebrates Native Americans in the community by holding its Festival of Native American Culture. It features Native American art, music, and dance.

Young people in this community are learning how to take care of a garden.

2. **Fill In** the chart with examples that describe your community.

My Community

Land Resources	Water Resources	Work	Activities

Communities Change Over Time

Think about when you were in kindergarten. Are you the same now? Of course not! You have grown and changed. Communities change over time, too. Sometimes the land changes. What was once an open field may be a parking lot today.

A small town could grow into a big city as more and more people make their homes there. New and different businesses open. A shop that sold farm supplies in the past may now be a computer store. A narrow road that was once for horses and wagons may now be a highway.

One thing has not changed over time: people in every kind of community want to make the community a better place. They might work at food banks or pick up litter to make their communities better places to live.

You can find out how your community was settled and how it has changed. Go to the local library or a nearby museum. Look for books, maps, poems, songs, photos, letters, and newspapers about your community. Interview people who have lived in your community for a long time. Find out about people who first settled there and people who have buildings and roads named after them. Tell the story of your community!

3. Circle something that is the same in both pictures.

Florida State Capitol, 1972

Florida State Capitol, present-day

4. ⊙ **Generalize Write** one fact that supports this generalization: People in a community want to help make it a better place.

....

....

....

....

5. ⊙ **Main Idea and Details Describe** two ways that communities can grow and change over time.

....

....

....

....

6. ⊙ **Write** about three jobs people in your community have.   my Story Ideas
Explain how these jobs make your community a better place.

....

....

....

....

■ **Stop!** I need help with ....

❚❚ **Wait!** I have a question about ....

▶ **Go!** Now I know ....

Generalize

A generalization is a broad statement that tells how different ideas or facts are alike in some way. Look at the chart below and read the three facts. Each fact tells a different way people use trees to meet their needs. Now read the generalization. The generalization is a statement made about all of the facts. It tells how the facts are alike: people use trees to meet their needs.

Fact

People use trees to get food they need.

Fact

People use trees for fuel they need.

Fact

People use trees to build houses they need.

Generalization
People use trees to meet their needs.

Read the newspaper article about Maple City.
Then **answer** the questions.

———— Maple City News ————

Soccer season starts this Saturday in Maple City! The town just finished building a new soccer field. Now there are two large soccer fields: one for the girls' team and one for the boys' team. Since there are two fields, each team has enough time to practice. People in the community also raised money to pay for new equipment and uniforms for both teams. Maple City is a great place to play soccer!

A soccer game in Maple City

1. **Underline** two facts about soccer in Maple City.

2. **Circle** the generalization in the article that tells how these facts are alike.

3. **Write** three facts to support this generalization:
   My community is a great place to live.

   ....

   ....

   ....

   ....

Where Communities Are Located

Envision It!

Look at the map. Draw a line to show how the bus gets to the library.

How can you find out where a community is located? People can use maps or a globe to find a community's location. In outer space, machines called satellites take pictures that can help locate communities. Many drivers use a global positioning system (GPS) in their cars to help them find communities they have never visited.

Parts of a Map

A map has many parts. The title of a map tells what the map shows. The title of the map on this page is Florida. The compass rose on this map shows **cardinal directions:** north (N), south (S), east (E), and west (W). A compass rose can also show intermediate directions. **Intermediate directions** are northeast (NE), southeast (SE), northwest (NW), and southwest (SW).

Maps can have symbols, too. Each **symbol** on a map stands for something. The map key, or legend, explains what the symbols stand for. Notice the map scale above the key on the map. A map scale shows how to measure the real distance between two places on a map.

1. Circle the compass rose on the map.

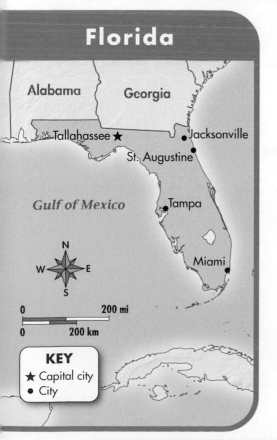

Florida

Alabama   Georgia

Tallahassee ★   ● Jacksonville
    St. Augustine ●

Gulf of Mexico   ● Tampa

N
W   E
S

● Miami

0   200 mi
0   200 km

KEY
★ Capital city
● City

Vocabulary

cardinal direction	relative location
intermediate direction	absolute location
symbol	hemisphere

Grid Maps

You can use a grid to find places on a map. A grid is a pattern of lines that forms squares. Each row of squares on a grid map has a letter, and each column of squares has a number.

Look at the grid map of Boston, Massachusetts. It shows features such as old buildings and monuments called landmarks. You can use the grid to help find the landmarks. Put your finger on the letter C. Then move your finger to the right into Box 2. That is where you will find the Paul Revere House: it is located at C-2. Where is Bunker Hill? What is the letter and number of the square? That's right! It is at A-1.

2. 🎯 **Main Idea and Details Explain** how to use a grid to find a place on a map.

....

....

....

....

Boston

KEY
— Freedom Trail
■ Landmark

Bunker Hill

USS Constitution

Charles River   0   1,000 ft

Old North Church

Paul Revere House

Boston Inner Harbor

Old State House

Absolute and Relative Location

You can describe the location of a place in two ways. You can say that Washington, D.C., is in the eastern part of the United States, along the Potomac River near Baltimore, Maryland. This is the **relative location**, or a description of where a place is in relation to other places. To describe the **absolute location**, you tell exactly where a place is located on Earth. You can find the absolute location of a place by using a map or globe. Lines of latitude and longitude are imaginary lines that can help you find the absolute location.

The equator is a line of latitude that divides Earth into two parts, or **hemispheres,** called the Northern and Southern hemispheres. The Tropic of Cancer and the Tropic of Capricorn are also lines of latitude. The prime meridian is a line of longitude that divides Earth into the Western and Eastern hemispheres. On the opposite side of Earth from the prime meridian is another imaginary line called the international date line.

3. **Circle** a city that is in the Southern Hemisphere. **Underline** a city that is in the Eastern Hemisphere.

The World

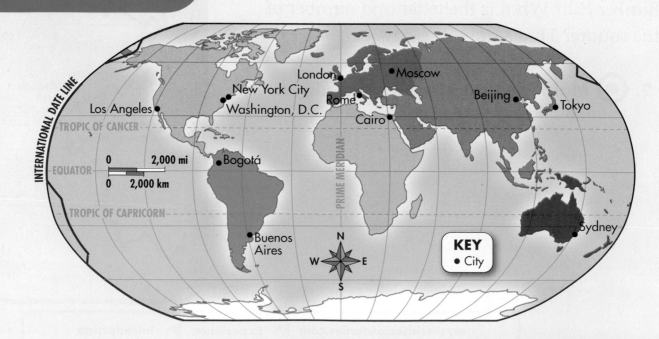

Measuring Distance

A map scale allows you to measure the real distances between places on a map.

How can you measure the real distance between two cities on a map? First, put a ruler just below the line on a map scale. Find out how many inches long the line is. Then, read the number on the map scale to tell how many miles 1 inch stands for. Next, use the ruler to measure the distance between the two cities. Be sure your ruler touches both cities. Then, count the number of inches between them. Finally, do the math. For example, if 1 inch stands for 600 miles, and there are 2 inches between cities, multiply 600 miles by 2 inches. Then you will find out that the actual distance between the cities is 1,200 miles.

I am located in New York City!

4. **Use** the map scale to **measure** the distance between Atlanta and Washington, D.C.

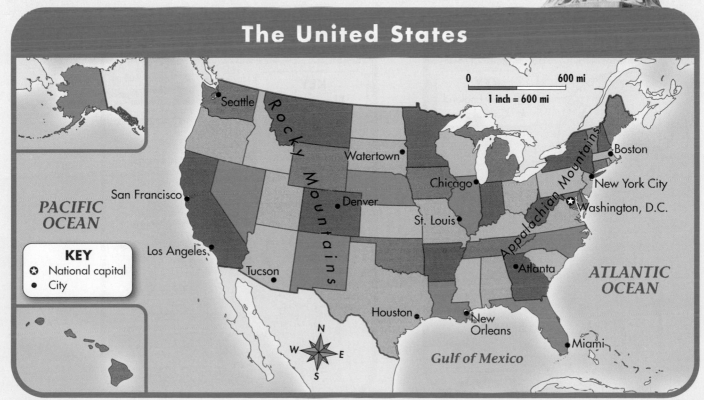

The United States

0   600 mi
1 inch = 600 mi

Seattle
Rocky Mountains
Watertown
San Francisco
PACIFIC OCEAN
Denver
Chicago
St. Louis
Boston
New York City
Washington, D.C.
Appalachian Mountains

KEY
⊗ National capital
• City

Los Angeles
Tucson
Houston
New Orleans
Atlanta
ATLANTIC OCEAN
Miami
Gulf of Mexico

N W E S

27

Different Types of Maps

There are many kinds of maps used for different purposes. When you take the round surface of Earth and make it flat on a map, distortion happens. When something is distorted, it looks different from its real size and shape. Remember this when you look at each type of map.

One type of map is a political map. A political map can show country and state boundaries, or borders. You can also find major cities and capitals on a political map.

Another type of map is a physical map. You can find valleys, mountains, plains, and deserts on a physical map. You can also find bodies of water, such as rivers, lakes, and oceans. Different colors are used on the map to show different land heights, or elevations. For example, valleys have lower elevations than mountains. Therefore, valleys are shaded in a different color than mountains. The map key tells which colors show lower and higher elevations.

Maps can help you find your way when you are hiking.

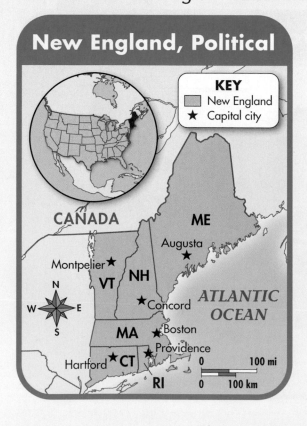

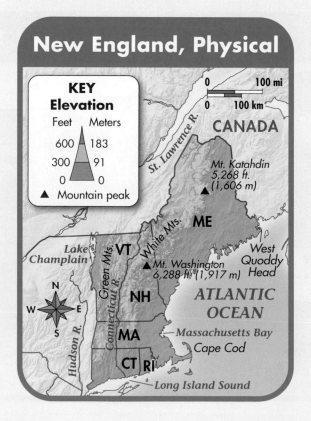

Population is the total number of people who live in a place. A population map shows the number of people living in certain areas. The map key shows that populations with different numbers of people are shaded in different colors.

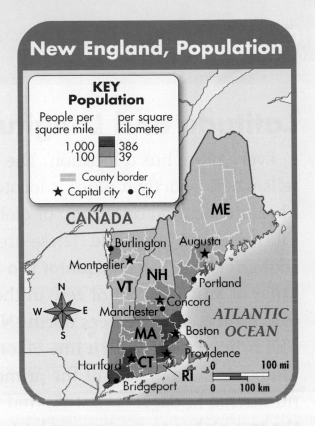

New England, Population

KEY
Population

People per square mile — per square kilometer

1,000 — 386
100 — 39

County border
★ Capital city • City

5. **Circle** one city that has a larger population than Concord.

6. **Find** a political map of North America and the Caribbean in an atlas. Then **use** that map to **label** the countries of North America and the Caribbean on an outline map.

Got it?

7. ◉ **Generalize** Different maps are used for different purposes. **Write** a sentence about what you learned that supports this generalization.

....

....

....

8. ❓ Suppose someone was looking for your community on a map. **Describe** the relative location of your community.

my Story Ideas

....

....

⬛ **Stop!** I need help with ....

⏸ **Wait!** I have a question about ....

▶ **Go!** Now I know ....

Latitude and Longitude

Every place has a location. The absolute location tells where exactly a place is located on Earth. To find absolute location on a map or globe, you use lines of latititude and longitude. These are imaginary lines that circle Earth. The equator is a line of latitude. Lines of latitude start at zero at the equator and are numbered in degrees north (N) and south (S). The prime meridian is a line of longitude. Lines of longitude start at zero at the prime meridian and are numbered in degrees east (E) and west (W). Look at the two globes to see lines of latitude and longitude.

Now look at the map below. Place your finger on New Orleans. Now look to see which lines of latitude and longitude are nearest to the city. That is New Orleans's absolute location. It is 30° N and 90° W.

Latitude

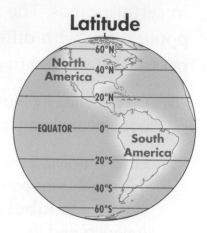

Longitude

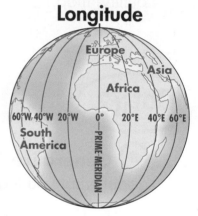

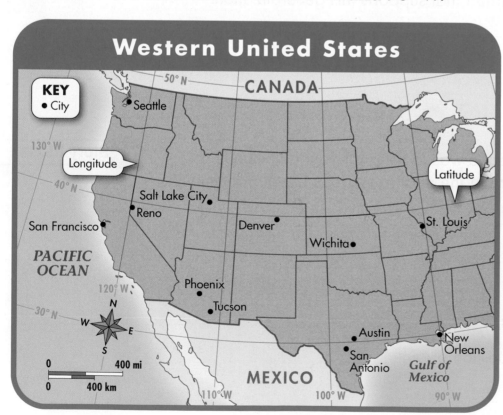

Western United States

Learning Objective

I will know how to find the absolute location of a place on a map.

Look at the map below. Then **answer** the questions.

1. **Write** which lines of latitude and longitude Pittsburgh is closest to.

   ....

2. **Circle** the city that is closest to 30° N and 80° W.

3. **Look** at the route from Boston to Little Rock. **Tell** which lines of latitude and longitude you would cross if you traveled along this route.

   ....

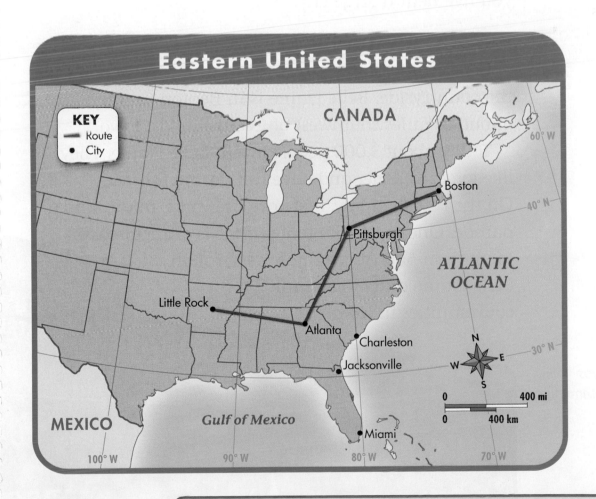

Eastern United States

Envision It!

□

□

Mark an X in the box next to the picture that shows the kind of community you live in.

What kind of community do you live in? If your community is in the countryside where there is plenty of open space, then you live in a **rural** community. If you live in a large city, you live in an **urban** community. If you live in a **suburban** community, you live near a large city.

Rural Communities

Belle Plaine, Iowa, is a rural community. It is in the countryside. Belle Plaine is in Benton County. It is about 40 miles southwest of Cedar Rapids, Iowa.

Today about 3,000 people live in Belle Plaine. They like to get together and have fun during the year. On the Fourth of July, there are fireworks, music, and a parade. One special kind of parade is a tractorcade. More than 500 tractors parade through Belle Plaine and other rural communities in Iowa!

A tractorcade moves through a rural community.

Vocabulary

rural
urban
suburban

Some people in rural communities work on farms and live in farmhouses. Farmers grow corn, wheat, and many other crops. People in larger towns and cities depend on these farms for fresh fruits and vegetables.

People in rural communities depend on other communities, too. They travel to suburban or urban communities. These communities have large malls, or places with many stores. People from rural communities can buy clothing, toys, and groceries they need in these stores.

1. **Write** about what you might see in a rural community.

   ....

   ....

   ....

You often see farms in rural communities.

Suburban Communities

Dale City, Virginia, is a suburban community. It is about 30 miles away from Washington, D.C. Dale City is located in Prince William County in the northern part of Virginia. Today about 71,000 people live in Dale City.

Like other suburban communities, there are many houses with yards lining the streets of Dale City. You can also expect to see a library, a post office, stores, a movie theater, and parks there. Take a short drive, and you will find a water park and a very large shopping mall.

People of Dale City are proud of their suburban community. When there is litter on the streets of Dale City, people help clean it up. They cut the grass and clean streets, just like people in other suburban communities around our country and the world do.

Dale City, Virginia

People work together to keep their community clean.

There are plenty of activities to keep children busy in Dale City. They can go for a swim at the community pool or play basketball in a local park. They can also join a baseball or soccer league.

Many people who live in suburban communities work in a nearby city. Some people who live in Dale City work in Washington, D.C. While some drive their cars or trucks on busy highways, others choose to take an express bus to work.

People began moving to suburban communities to get away from the crowded cities. New highways helped suburban communities grow. People could get to the city safely and quickly, so living in the suburbs became more popular. Highways made coming back from the city easy, too. Get off at an exit and you are almost home!

2. ⊙ **Generalize List** two facts that support this generalization: There are many activities that children in Dale City can enjoy.

....

....

....

People in suburbs use highways to get to and from the city.

Urban Communities

Many people live, work, and play in urban communities like San Francisco, California. Today about 800,000 people live in San Francisco. Most live in apartment buildings and row houses. Row houses share walls. In San Francisco and other cities, people work in tall buildings, or skyscrapers.

Many people from suburban communities travel to San Francisco to work. They may also come to shop in stores, visit museums, and eat at restaurants. Some travel to San Francisco across the Golden Gate Bridge by car or bus. Others ride ferryboats. Once inside the city, people can ride cable cars through San Francisco's hilly streets.

San Francisco

3. ◎ **Compare and Contrast Underline** the words in the chart that show how the population in each type of community is different.

Features of Communities

	Rural	Suburban	Urban
Location	in the countryside	near a large city	in a large city
Population	small population	medium-sized population	large population
Buildings	farmhouses, barns	houses, shopping malls	apartment buildings, row houses, skyscrapers

4. ◉ **Generalize Write** a generalization about an urban community. Then **write** two facts to support your generalization.

....

....

....

....

....

....

5. ② **Describe** the type of community you live in. **Explain** how your community is similar to and different from one of the other types of communities.

my Story Ideas

....

....

....

....

....

◻ **Stop!** I need help with ....

❚❚ **Wait!** I have a question about ....

▶ **Go!** Now I know ....

Review and Assessment

Lesson 1

What Makes a Community?

1. Draw a picture that shows how a community can change over time.

Then   **Now**

2. ⊙ **Generalize Read** the three facts. Then **circle** the generalization that can be made about these facts.

Facts
- People work together in communities.

- People have fun together in communities.

- People help each other in communities.

Generalizations
- Communities have many people.

- People make communities special places to live.

- People farm in some communities.

Review and Assessment

Where Communities Are Located

3. List three things you find on a political map.

....

....

....

....

4. Look at the political map of Oklahoma. **Circle** the capital city of Oklahoma. **Underline** the city southeast of the capital.

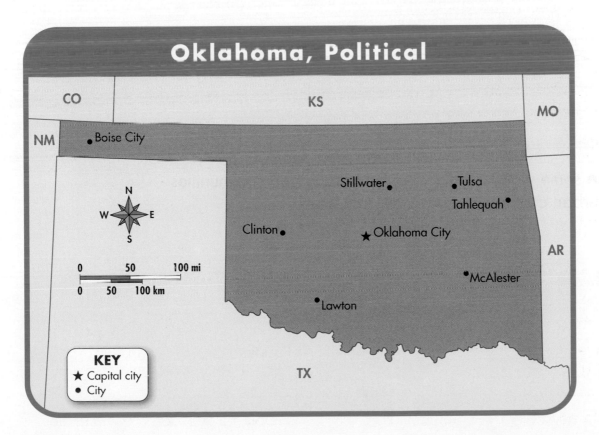

Oklahoma, Political

CO
KS
MO
NM
• Boise City

Stillwater •
• Tulsa
Tahlequah •

Clinton •
★ Oklahoma City

AR

N
W E
S

0   50   100 mi
0   50   100 km

• McAlester

• Lawton

TX

KEY
★ Capital city
• City

Review and Assessment

Three Types of Communities

5. Fill in the circle next to the correct answer.

In a rural community, which would you most likely see?

○ tall buildings

○ farms

○ an amusement park

○ a subway

6. List three activities people can do for fun in a suburban community.

....

....

....

....

7. Describe some ways people who live in suburban communities travel to urban communities like San Francisco.

....

....

....

....

Go online to write and illustrate your own **myStory Book** using the **myStory Ideas** from this chapter.

 What makes a good community?

In this chapter, you have learned about communities and where they are located. People live in rural, suburban, and urban communities. In each type of community, people work together to make it a better place to live.

Think about your community. **Write** about what you can do to make it a better place to live.

....

....

....

....

Now **draw** a picture of people in your community who work to make it a better place to live.

While you're online, check out **myStory Current Events** area where you can create your own book on a topic that's in the news.

Our Environment

How do we interact with our planet?

Think about your surroundings. Then **describe** the land and water features and the weather.

....

....

....

....

Jacques-Yves Cousteau
Underwater Adventurer

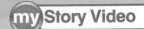

People need oceans, lakes, and rivers to live. People rely on them for fresh drinking water, food, and transportation. Even though people have always used these bodies of water, few people knew much about what was beneath the surface of the water until the 1930s. Jacques-Yves Cousteau [zhahk eev koo STOH] changed that.

In the 1930s, Cousteau began to examine the sea life underwater. He put on his goggles, held his breath, and swam. However, Cousteau wanted to go deeper into the ocean. He also wanted to swim for longer periods of time. Cousteau worked with Émile Gagnan to make an underwater breathing machine called the Aqua-Lung™. It could be worn on a person's back while swimming. It allowed Cousteau to swim into deeper waters and breathe for longer periods of time.

Cousteau soon traveled to different oceans. He wanted to share what he found underwater. With help, he developed an underwater camera that could take pictures of what he saw.

Cousteau wore a diving suit and a breathing machine.

43

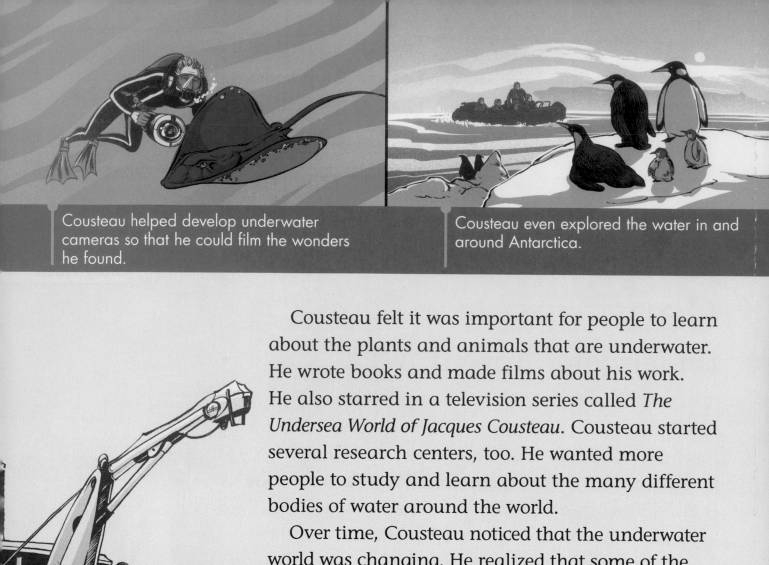

Cousteau helped develop underwater cameras so that he could film the wonders he found.

Cousteau even explored the water in and around Antarctica.

Cousteau felt it was important for people to learn about the plants and animals that are underwater. He wrote books and made films about his work. He also starred in a television series called *The Undersea World of Jacques Cousteau*. Cousteau started several research centers, too. He wanted more people to study and learn about the many different bodies of water around the world.

Over time, Cousteau noticed that the underwater world was changing. He realized that some of the things that people did affected sea life. He wanted to protect the oceans. He also wanted to take action to repair some of the damage people had done.

Cousteau and his crew traveled underwater in what was called a diving saucer.

Cousteau began to see changes that showed that the underwater world was being harmed.

Cousteau told world leaders that we need to protect our oceans.

In the early 1970s, Cousteau started The Cousteau Society. He organized this group to help protect the sea life that was being harmed by people's actions. Today, there are more than 50,000 members. The Cousteau Society continues to study the oceans and to work to protect them. It also teaches others about the oceans.

All over the world, there are natural and man-made landmarks that help keep Cousteau's vision alive. The Barrier Reef Reserve System in Belize is home to many threatened animals. People continue to explore sea life there. At the Vancouver Aquarium in Canada, people protect sea life and help sick or injured animals become healthy again.

Think About It Based on this story, why do you think it is important to protect the oceans? As you read the chapter ahead, think about how people can affect and change the land and water.

Lesson 1

Land and Water

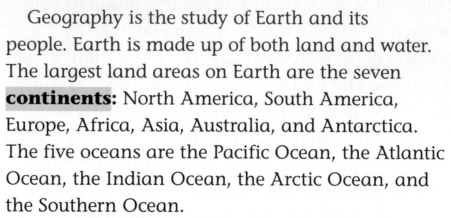

Glacier

Island

Peninsula

Geography is the study of Earth and its people. Earth is made up of both land and water. The largest land areas on Earth are the seven **continents:** North America, South America, Europe, Africa, Asia, Australia, and Antarctica. The five oceans are the Pacific Ocean, the Atlantic Ocean, the Indian Ocean, the Arctic Ocean, and the Southern Ocean.

Landforms and Bodies of Water

There are many different landforms on each of the seven continents. A **landform** is the form or shape of part of Earth's surface.

Glaciers, mountains, hills, islands, and peninsulas are landforms. Glaciers are made up of ice and snow. Mountains are land masses that rise above the surrounding land. Some mountains are rounded at the top while others form a rocky peak. Hills are usually lower than mountains and have rounded tops. Islands are areas of land surrounded on all sides by water. Peninsulas are connected to a mainland and are nearly surrounded by water. There is usually water on only three sides of a peninsula.

46

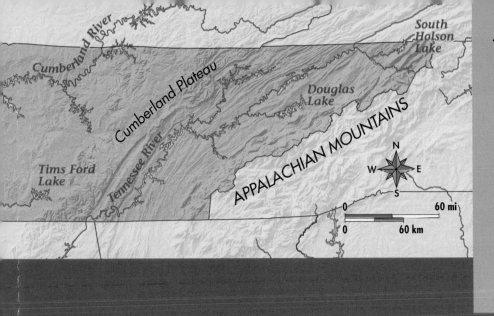

Vocabulary

continent
landform
mine
adobe

Just like landforms, bodies of water are all different shapes and sizes. On the map, find the five oceans. Oceans are the largest bodies of salt water on Earth. Lakes and rivers provide people with freshwater. The Great Lakes in the United States are the largest freshwater lakes in the world. These lakes include Lake Superior, Lake Michigan, Lake Huron, Lake Erie, and Lake Ontario.

1. **Circle** a landform in North America. **Underline** the body of water north of Asia.

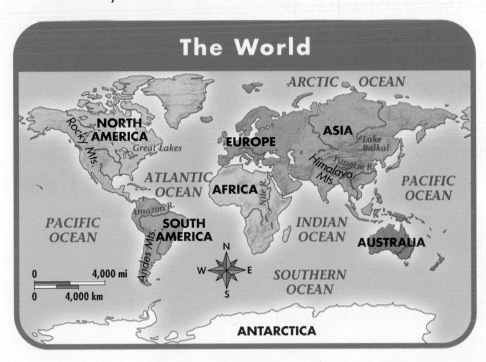

The World

Land and Water in the United States

Geographers who study land areas often organize the United States into regions. The states in each region are grouped based on their location and the landforms they share. The United States is organized into five regions: the West, the Midwest, the Northeast, the Southeast, and the Southwest.

Many different landforms are found in the regions of the United States. The Appalachian Mountains stretch across the Southeast and Northeast regions. In between mountains there are low areas called valleys. Plains, such as the Great Plains, are also low areas. They tend to be very flat. The Great Plains cover parts of the Midwest, Southwest, and West regions. Plateaus, such as the Columbia Plateau located in the West region, are high areas that have steep sides and flat tops. Mountains are also found in the West region.

The West region

The largest bodies of water in the United States are rivers and lakes. Locate the Mississippi River on the map. More than 2,000 miles long, it is the second longest river in the United States. It runs through the Midwest and Southeast regions. The Great Lakes, in the Midwest and Northeast regions, form part of the border between Canada and the United States.

2. **Look** at the map on the next page. **Label** the states in each of the five U.S. regions.

The Southwest region

The Northeast region

The Midwest region

United States Regions

Columbia Plateau

Rocky Mountains

Great Plains

Great Lakes

Mississippi R.

Ohio R.

Appalachian Mts.

ATLANTIC OCEAN

PACIFIC OCEAN

Rio Grande

KEY
- Northeast region
- Midwest region
- Southeast region
- Southwest region
- West region

The Southeast region

Five Regions of the United States

The Northeast region has some of the largest cities in the United States, such as New York City in New York, and Philadelphia, Pennsylvania. This region has areas of hills, rocky coastlines, and farmland. Many people also fish along the coast. Coasts are areas of flat land that are located near water.

This plantation home was built in the Southeast region in the early 1800s.

Early settlers in the Southeast region built large farms called plantations. However, the region is best known for its long coastlines today. Along the coasts, people fish, enjoy the warm weather, and visit the beaches. Farther inland, many people farm the rich soil.

The Midwest region is one of the flattest areas in the United States. In this region, many people work on farms. Other people **mine,** or dig for materials, such as coal and iron.

Many states in the Southwest region were once a part of Mexico. The deserts of this region are home to many Native Americans. Long ago, early settlers and Native Americans used sun-dried bricks called **adobe** [uh DOH bee] to build shelters and other buildings. In the Southwest today, people still build with adobe.

Homes made of adobe are found in the Southwest region.

The West is a region of mountains. The Rocky Mountains are in this region. They are some of the tallest mountains in the United States. Other mountain ranges include the Coast Ranges and the Alaska Range. The West region also has a long coast. Many people visit the West to hike, fish, and camp. People also come to visit the beaches.

3. ⊙ **Cause and Effect Explain** what might cause people in a region to work as farmers.

....

....

....

....

....

Most of the corn in the United States is grown in the Midwest region.

Got it?

4. ⊙ **Cause and Effect Choose** one region of the United States. **Write** about how the landforms may affect some of the activities people do. **Look** for clues in the maps and photographs.

....

....

....

5. ❓ **Describe** the landforms and bodies of water that you live near. **Write** about how they affect the activities you do.

my Story Ideas

....

....

....

⏹ **Stop!** I need help with ....

⏸ **Wait!** I have a question about ....

▶ **Go!** Now I know ....

Weather and Climate

Polar bears live in areas that are cold.

Alligators live in areas that are wet.

Draw an animal you like. Add details that show the weather where the animal lives.

This rain forest is in a warm and wet climate. Plants grow here all year.

What is the weather today? When you explain the **weather,** you tell about the daily conditions outside. It may be hot, rainy, or cold. **Climate** is the weather that a place has over a long period. There are three parts that make up the climate of a region: temperature, precipitation, and wind. Temperature is how hot or cold it is. Precipitation is the amount of rain or snow that falls.

Climate Regions

Climates are different from region to region. In fact, the climate of a region depends on its location on Earth. Places located close to the equator get more direct sunlight. Places far from the equator get less direct sunlight.

Bodies of water shape the climate of places near them. They affect the amount of rain that falls. Bodies of water also change the temperature since they warm and cool more slowly than land. In summer, winds that blow from the water cool the land. In winter, the winds that blow from the water warm the land. The **elevation,** or the height of land above sea level, affects climate, too. High places and mountains are cool most of the year.

Vocabulary

weather   vegetation
climate   ecosystem
elevation

The map of North America shows the different climate regions on the continent. Arctic climates are cool or cold most of the year. Tropical climates are wet and hot most of the year. Temperate climates are not as cold as arctic climates or as hot as tropical climates. Most of the United States is in a temperate climate region. However, parts of the West have dry desert climates. In the desert, there is little rainfall. The temperature during the day can be hot while the temperature at night can be cold.

1. **Look** at the map. **Write** the climate found in most of Canada.

....

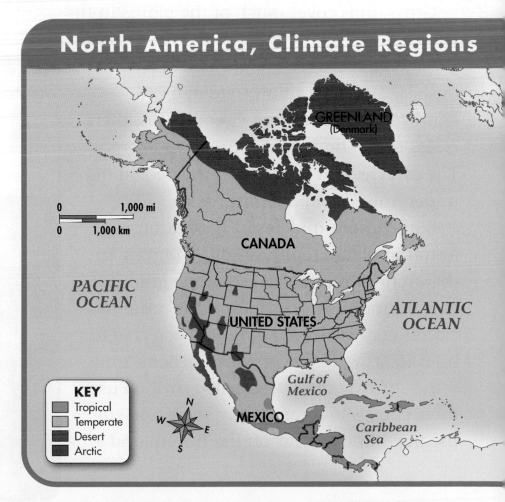

North America, Climate Regions

GREENLAND (Denmark)

CANADA

PACIFIC OCEAN

UNITED STATES

ATLANTIC OCEAN

Gulf of Mexico

MEXICO

Caribbean Sea

0   1,000 mi
0   1,000 km

KEY
- Tropical
- Temperate
- Desert
- Arctic

N W E S

Climate and Plants

The climate of a place affects the plants that grow there. Both the temperature and the amount of rainfall determine the types of **vegetation**, or kinds of plant life, that grow. In the United States there are four main types of vegetation: forests, grasslands, tundra, and deserts. Different animals depend on the vegetation that grows in an area.

In climate regions that have plenty of rainfall, large forests are found. Forests grow in many parts of the United States. In fact, not long ago, forests covered most of North America! Many forests today are found in parts of the West region, near the Great Lakes, and in the eastern United States. Animals such as bears, deer, and raccoons live in forests.

Grasslands cover much of the plains in the United States. Some parts of the Great Plains get enough rain for tall grasses, berry bushes, and even small trees to grow. However, in the western Great Plains, there is less rain. Short grasses are found here. The prairie dogs that live in this region dig underground and eat the grasses.

Both tundra and desert vegetation are found in places that have dry climates. In the arctic climates of Alaska, the land is called tundra. In the tundra, the ground is frozen nearly all year long. It is too cold for trees to grow. However, moss, lichens, and some shrubs grow. Deer called caribou use their hooves to scrape away snow and eat the moss and lichens off the frozen land.

In parts of Alaska, shrubs and moss grow in the tundra.

In desert climates the only plants that can survive are those that can live with little water. In some deserts, grasses and shrubs are found. In the deserts of the West region, there are large cactuses called saguaros [suh GWAR ohs]. Saguaros grow in Mexico, too. Saguaros have long roots that allow them to get water from a wide area. A saguaro can grow to be 50 feet high. That is nearly as tall as a five-story building!

Animals that live in deserts can survive the hot temperatures during the day. Some animals, such as desert tortoises, keep cool by spending much of their time underground. Other animals only come out at night when it is cooler.

2. **Main Idea and Details** Fill in each box with two details about each type of vegetation.

Forests	Grasslands

Tundra	Desert

The plants that grow in the desert need only small amounts of water.

Plants and Animals Work Together

Forests, deserts, and grasslands each have different ecosystems. In an **ecosystem** all living things, such as the plants and animals, interact with each other.

In both forest and rain forest ecosystems, birds, squirrels, and other animals depend on trees. Birds and other animals build nests in trees. They also eat the fruits and nuts that grow on trees. Some of the seeds the animals eat drop into the soil and grow into new trees. The vegetation in these ecosystems needs animals to help spread the seeds around.

Lesser long-nosed bat

In the desert, cactuses are important to many animals. Bats, such as the lesser long-nosed bats, drink nectar from the cactus flowers that bloom at night. By doing this, the bats spread pollen from cactus to cactus. This helps the cactus fruit grow. Birds also make nests in dried cactus limbs. Other animals, including jack rabbits, eat parts of the cactus.

Places with similar vegetation can have different ecosystems. The grasslands in the middle of the United States do not have the same ecosystem as the grasslands on the continent of Africa. Some of the grasslands in Africa get more rainfall. The grasses can even grow up to seven feet high there! In this ecosystem, elephants eat the tall grasses.

Jack rabbit

In the lake and swamp ecosystems in the southeastern United States, alligators dig large pond-like holes. Alligators use the holes as a place to rest. The holes also provide shallow water for birds and fish.

3. ⊙ **Cause and Effect** **Choose** one ecosystem.
Explain the effect the animals have on the
vegetation there.

....

....

....

....

....

Got it?

4. ⊙ **Cause and Effect** **Explain** the effect the climate has on vegetation
that grows in a region.

....

....

5. ❓ **Write** about how the weather or climate affects
how you live.

....

....

....

....

⏹ **Stop!** I need help with ....

⏸ **Wait!** I have a question about ....

▶ **Go!** Now I know ....

Map Skills

Interpret Maps

Maps can show different types of information. Maps that show details about the land are physical maps. On elevation maps, colors are used to show how high the land is above the surface of the sea, or sea level.

On the elevation map, place your finger on the West Coast. Move your finger across the map toward the East. The Rocky Mountains are mostly shaded in purple and brown. The map key shows that land shaded in purple has an elevation higher than 10,000 feet above sea level. Land shaded in brown has an elevation between 6,000 and 10,000 feet above sea level.

United States Elevation

KEY
Elevation

Feet	Meters
10,000	3,048
6,000	1,829
3,000	914
1,000	305
500	152
0	0

★ National capital
• City
▲ Peak

The Great Plains is mostly shaded in yellow. This means that the elevation is 1,000 to 3,000 feet above sea level. On the East Coast, most of the land is shaded dark green. Therefore, the elevation of the land is between 0 and 500 feet above sea level.

Read the elevation map. Then answer the questions.

1. **Look** at the map key. **Write** the color that shows elevation between 500 and 1,000 feet above sea level.

....

2. **Find** the Appalachian Mountains in the East. **Write** the elevation of most of the Appalachian Mountains.

....

....

3. **Find** Orlando, Florida. Then **write** its elevation.

....

....

4. **Write** how you can tell the elevation of an area of land.

....

....

....

Using Earth's Resources

Envision It!

Water is important to all living things. Write how you use water.

Earth has many different natural resources. Some natural resources, such as soil and trees, are found on the land. Other natural resources are minerals like gold and iron. Water is another important natural resource. People use water to meet many of their needs.

Natural Resources

There are many natural resources in North America. Canada has many minerals, forests, and rich soil. Iron and gold are natural resources found in Mexico. Oil can be found in Trinidad and Tobago, and there are forests and rich soil throughout the Caribbean islands.

In parts of the West region of the United States, there are forests. In other parts, there is rich soil. Animals can eat the grasses that grow in the drier areas. The West also has minerals such as gold.

In the Southwest region the land is used for mining and to raise animals such as cows. Oil, a natural resource used for fuel, is also found in the region. This natural resource is found in parts of Oklahoma and Texas.

People need rich soil to grow food.

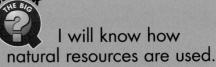

I will know how natural resources are used.

Vocabulary

agricultural region

industrial region

renewable resource

nonrenewable resource

conserve

erosion

recycle

There is rich soil in parts of the Midwest, Northeast, and Southeast regions. Many crops are grown in these regions. You can see on the map that coal is also found in all three of these regions. Iron is found in the northern part of the Midwest region.

1. Circle three types of natural resources in the West.

United States Resources

West Region

Midwest Region

Northeast Region

Southwest Region

Southeast Region

0   400 mi
0   400 km

West Region

0   100 mi
0   100 km

0   250 mi
0   250 km

KEY

Agricultural area
Industrial area
Other uses
— Region border
Oil
Coal
Iron
Gold
Timber

Agriculture and Products

People use natural resources to make products they need. In an **agricultural region**, or a place where there is much flat land and rich soil, people use the land and soil to farm.

Farmers grow many different crops. The top five crops grown in the United States are corn, soybeans, hay, wheat, and cotton. Some crops are grown for people to eat, and some are made into products. Cotton is made into fabric for clothing. People buy plastic containers and car seats made from soybeans.

Cotton

In other agricultural regions, vegetable and fruit crops are grown for people to eat. People also use grasses to feed animals such as cows and sheep.

People make other products from the natural resources that grow on the land. In some forest regions, people cut down trees. The trees are then sent to mills and made into timber, or lumber, for building. Wood from trees is also turned into pulp to make paper products.

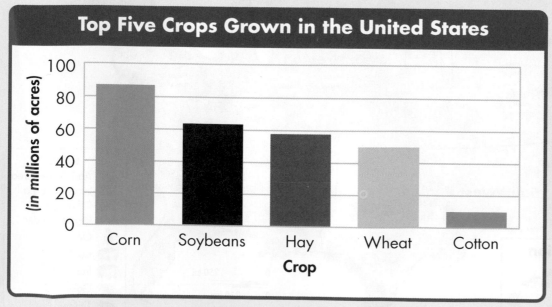

Top Five Crops Grown in the United States

(in millions of acres) — Crop: Corn, Soybeans, Hay, Wheat, Cotton

Source: U.S. Department of Agriculture, National Agricultural Statistics Service, 2007

Industry and Products

People make products from the resources found underground, too. Many of these products are made in industrial regions. An **industrial region** is a place where many kinds of factories are located. In the United States, many industrial regions are located near large cities such as Chicago, Illinois, and Detroit, Michigan.

Gasoline is made from oil.

In many places with oil and natural gas, people pump them from underground. The oil is then made into fuel such as gasoline. Oil can also be heated to make plastic. Then the plastic is used to make many different products such as telephones, plastic bags, and even toys! Most people use gasoline to power automobiles. They also use gas or oil to heat their water and their homes. People mine coal, copper, zinc, and iron. Coal is used to help make electricity. Coins, including pennies, are made from copper and zinc. Iron is used to make steel. Steel is used in making automobiles and building materials.

Minerals are melted to make items such as coins.

2. **Look** at the chart. **Write** a natural resource used to make or grow each pair of products.

Products	vegetables wheat	lumber paper	telephones toys
Natural Resource			

63

Protecting Resources

Some resources people use, such as trees and soil, are renewable resources. A **renewable resource** is one that can be replaced in a short time. Many of the resources found underground are nonrenewable resources.

Recycled materials can be used again.

Nonrenewable resources are those that take a long time to replace or cannot be replaced after they are used. Coal, oil, and natural gas are all nonrenewable resources. In order to make sure that everyone has enough natural resources to live, people find ways to **conserve**, or to save and protect, them.

One way people conserve resources is by using less of them. Many people try to use less natural gas or water. People also conserve resources when they use them more carefully. Some farmers plant trees near their crops or strips of grass in between rows of crops. These plants help prevent **erosion,** or the washing away of soil by rain, wind, and nearby rivers. The plants help to hold the soil down.

Another way to protect natural resources is by recycling them. To **recycle** means to use an item again. Plastic bottles, newspapers, aluminum cans, and glass bottles are all items that people recycle every day. In many neighborhoods, trucks pick up these items from bins that line the streets. Many factories use recycled materials instead of natural resources to make new products.

People conserve water when they turn off the faucet while they brush their teeth.

64

While many people work hard to protect natural resources, sometimes people's actions can harm them. Chemicals used in factories and on farms can pollute the air and nearby waterways. Smoke from burning fires can also pollute the air.

3. ⊙ **Cause and Effect Write** an effect of recycling items you use every day.

....

....

....

4. ⊙ **Cause and Effect Describe** a cause of pollution.

....

....

....

5. ❓ **Think** about your daily routine. **Describe** which natural resources you use the most.

my Story Ideas

....

....

....

⬛ **Stop!** I need help with ....

⏸ **Wait!** I have a question about ....

▶ **Go!** Now I know ....

Cause and Effect

One way to learn more about what you have read is to identify a cause and its effect. A cause makes something happen. An effect is the outcome, or the result of what happens. Sometimes writers use the words *cause* and *effect* to show readers how events are related. Other words, such as *because, if, then, now,* and *since,* help you identify examples of cause and effect.

Read the passage below to identify the causes and effects. Be sure to look for key words that signal a cause or effect.

Cause

Lily sees that a storm is coming! Soon, she sees the cracks of lightning and hears a loud "pop." Lightning has struck the electricity pole on the street. Now there is no electricity in her house. Since the electricity is out, the television, the radio, and the refrigerator are off. Hours later, after the storm passes, Lily decides to get a snack. She opens the refrigerator. "Oh no!" she says. Because the electricity went out, the refrigerator was off. Now the ice cream has melted!

Effect

Look at the phrases and sentences that are highlighted. The causes in the passage are highlighted orange. The effects are highlighted purple. Notice that the words *since* and *because* help you identify causes. The word *now* signals the effects.

Read the passage below. Then answer the questions.

For many years, groups of people drilled for oil at Spindletop in Texas. Then one group of workers got a new part for their drill. They were now able to dig deeper into the ground. On January 10, 1901, mud began to bubble up from the well. Then suddenly a stream of oil shot up more than 100 feet high! The nearby city of Beaumont was changed forever. Since oil had been found near it, people from all over the country rushed to Beaumont in search of oil. The number of people living in Beaumont rose from 10,000 to 50,000 people. Now that there was plenty of oil, automobiles and factories started to use more of this natural resource.

1. **Circle** the causes in the passage.

2. **List** words that helped you identify the causes.

   ....

3. **Underline** the effects in the passage.

4. **Explain** what caused the population of Beaumont to grow to 50,000 people.

   ....

   ....

   ....

Interacting With the Environment

Write some of the ways people use lakes and the land near lakes.

Think about what makes up your environment. Landforms, bodies of water, vegetation, natural resources, and climate are all things that make up the environment of a place.

The Environment Affects People

The environment affects where people live, work, and play. Most communities develop in regions where there is plenty of land and fresh water. People also settle communities near natural resources. People live near forests to cut and plant trees. Other people live near the coast to fish. In the mountains and in desert areas, there are fewer settlements. These places do not always have flat land or enough water to grow crops.

People adapt to the environment to fit their needs. To **adapt** is to change the way you do something. People may change the way they dress or how they travel. In arctic climates, people dress in warm clothes to protect themselves from the cold. They ski or sled to travel down snow-covered hills. People drive snowmobiles in areas where it is difficult or unsafe to drive automobiles.

In arctic climates, people drive snowmobiles to get from place to place.

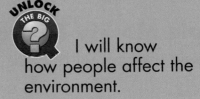

I will know how people affect the environment.

Vocabulary
....
adapt
modify
irrigate

People in states such as Texas and Florida, and in the countries of Central America, have changed how they make buildings. In these areas, heavy rains and hurricanes can bring strong winds and a quick rise in the water level. Many people in these places use building materials that can stay up in strong winds. Other people in these areas settle farther inland to avoid rising waters.

In Arizona, Native Americans called Havasupais [hah vah SOO pyez] live in a village in the Grand Canyon. This environment affects how they travel in and out of their village. People cannot drive automobiles down the canyon. Mail and other supplies are carried into the village on horseback or are flown in by helicopter.

1. ⊙ **Cause and Effect Describe** an effect of living in a cold, snowy climate.

....

....

....

The Havasupais live in the Grand Canyon.

People Modify Environments

People interact with, or act on, their environment in many ways. One way is to modify their environment to fit their needs. To **modify** is to change something, such as the physical environment. In areas with dry land, farmers may not have enough water for their crops. These farmers **irrigate**, or bring water in through pipes. Other farmers break up the soil to expose it to the air. This helps to kill weeds and to keep the soil rich. Farmers may add chemicals to the soil. Some are fertilizers that help farmers grow more crops. Other chemicals get rid of insects.

People modify the land when they use other natural resources, too. Large machines pump oil from the earth. In Pennsylvania and West Virginia, miners dig tunnels deep underground to reach minerals. Miners also carry away soil and rock to uncover coal. Land in some forests is cleared as workers cut down trees to sell as lumber. In some countries, people also burn forest areas to clear land. This land is used for farms or homes.

The areas near these resources have also been modified. People move to the area to work. They build homes and buildings they need. They also build roads, bridges, and railroads.

People modify rivers when they build dams. Dams are built across rivers to block the flow of the water. Gates on the dams allow some water to flow through. This water forms lakes behind the dams. People use the lakes for many activities, such as fishing or swimming. The water in these lakes may also be used to irrigate nearby farms. The rushing water that passes through some dams is used to make electricity.

In the United States, water from the Hoover Dam on the Colorado River is used to make electricity.

Effects of Population

The number of people who live in an area can also affect the physical environment. In the late 1800s and early 1900s, new tools and equipment made farming easier. Fewer farm workers were needed. Many people began to move to cities in the East to work in factories. As more people moved to cities, more space was needed for people to live.

As newcomers arrived, people built out from the center of the city. People built homes and other buildings they needed. They laid railroad tracks and built roads so people could travel in and out of the city. People also built upwards. They built tall buildings called skyscrapers. Over time, people used improved materials to build skyscrapers that were much taller.

Today, in areas with large populations, people modify the land to meet the changing needs in a community. As more people move to a city, more methods of transportation are added. The city may work on roads to make them wider so they can fit more cars, trucks, and buses. It might also build more rail lines so that more trains can travel into and out of the city. Builders may also build taller buildings so more people can live in the area.

2. Write two ways that people modify the land.

....

....

....

More people can live and work in large skyscrapers.

People and the Land

Some of the activities that people do can help or harm the environment. Scientists and others look for ways to improve the environment and how resources are used. Over the years, farmers learned that planting the same crops every year can harm the soil. As a result, many farmers today rotate, or take turns, growing different crops. Farmers also plan for a period of rest when they do not plant any crops. By doing so, the soil is moist and better able to grow crops.

Miners also work to help the environment. After they carve out soil in search of minerals, the land has little or no vegetation left. Miners then work to plant trees and other vegetation on the land.

Community leaders help the environment with some of the decisions they make. Leaders pass laws to prevent people from throwing garbage on the ground. They also pass laws to keep the drinking water clean. Some laws protect the oceans. These laws do not allow companies to dump materials that can harm the ocean or sea life.

Other people help the environment by their actions every day. Some people buy automobiles that do not pollute the air. People also use the heat from the sun or the wind to power things. Others organize groups to help clean up beaches, parks, and lakes. When people clean up the land, they make it safe for people and animals.

Cleaning up the land is one way people help the environment.

Another way people help the environment is by conserving land. People conserve land when they set aside some of it in state parks or national parks. The first national park was created in 1872. Today, there are more than 350 national parks in the United States. This land is protected. People may not build or settle on this land.

Yellowstone was the first national park.

3. **List** three ways people help the environment.

....

....

....

Got it?

4. ◎ **Cause and Effect Explain** the effect of a law that helps the environment.

....

....

....

5. ❓ **Describe** ways the land has been modified in your community.

....

....

....

⬛ **Stop!** I need help with ....

⏸ **Wait!** I have a question about ....

▶ **Go!** Now I know ....

Chapter 2
Review and Assessment

Lesson 1
Land and Water

1. Write the name of each landform under its picture.

2. Label the continents and oceans on the map below.

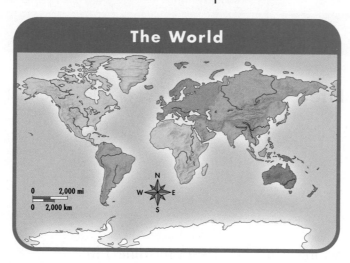

The World

Lesson 2
Weather and Climate

3. Describe two ways people can adapt to the climate of deserts in the West.

74

Review and Assessment

Lesson 3

Using Earth's Resources

4. **Write** what many people do for work in an agricultural region.

....

....

....

5. ◉ **Cause and Effect** Factories use natural resources to make products. **Describe** one effect of factories on the environment.

....

....

6. **Draw** a picture of something you have at home that is made from a natural resource. Then **write** the natural resource used to make it.

....

Lesson 4

Interacting With the Environment

7. Describe how people in Texas and Florida have changed how they make buildings.

....

....

....

8. Write why people may settle near a dam.

....

....

....

9. Explain what might happen if people cut down trees but did not plant new ones.

....

....

....

....

10. Fill in the circle next to the correct answer.

Which sentence describes what happens when there is erosion?

○ People move from the farm to the city.

○ New trees are planted in forests.

○ Farmers water their crops daily.

○ Soil is washed away by wind and rain.

Go online to write and illustrate your own **myStory Book** using the **myStory Ideas** from this chapter.

How do we interact with our planet?

Every day, people interact with their environment. In some ways, people may harm the land. In other ways, they help the land.

Think about how you interact with your environment. Then **write** about activities you can do to use fewer natural resources.

....

....

....

Draw a picture of someone doing an activity to help the environment.

While you're online, check out the **myStory Current Events** area where you can create your own book on a topic that's in the news.

Communities Build a Nation

How does our past affect our present?

Describe something about your community that is special.

....

....

....

....

....

The church at Mission San Luis

Mission San Luis
A Multicultural Community

my Story Video

From about 1560 to 1690, there were more than 100 Spanish missions built throughout Florida. A mission is a settlement that has a church where religion is taught. One of the most famous missions is Mission San Luis. Located in Tallahassee, it is one of the last remaining mission sites today. "It's also the only place where both the Apalachee and the Spaniards lived together," says Grace. The Apalachee are Native Americans and Spaniards are people from Spain. "I love learning about other cultures," she adds. No one lives at the mission anymore, but it has been rebuilt. Visitors can tour the mission and watch people act out what life was like there hundreds of years ago.

Grace was excited to visit one of the last remaining missions.

"Native Americans and Spaniards shared this mission," Grace explains. At that time, Native Americans and European settlers usually did not live together. Mission San Luis was special.

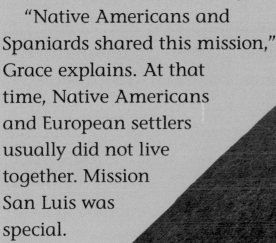

79

Squash and beans are some of the crops that the Apalachee used to grow.

The Spaniards built a fort to protect their settlement.

People working at the mission wear clothing from the time period as part of their teaching about life long ago.

The Apalachee were the first Americans to settle in this area. There was a river nearby and rich soil, which made it a good place to live. Over the years, the Apalachee learned a lot about farming and grew crops including corn, beans, and squash. *"Mi abuela* grows these crops, too!" says Grace. "Sorry, *abuela* means 'Grandma' in Spanish!" Grace and her family are originally from Puerto Rico, so English is Grace's second language. She uses a lot of Spanish words when she speaks. "Grandma says that our family has grown these crops for a long time, too," Grace tells us.

When the Spaniards came to the Florida coast, they were looking for a place where they could create a community, build a fort to protect the settlement, and spread their Christian religion. The Apalachee wanted to learn about Christianity, and they felt that the Spaniards could help protect them. So, the Apalachee welcomed the Spaniards to the area. By living together, both groups shared different ways of doing things and grew to respect each other's differences. "My family and I also learned a lot of new things when we came to America," Grace says. While most missions began to shrink during that time, San Luis grew.

This bedroom is decorated with Spanish fabrics.

Grace saw several Spanish artifacts in this dining area.

In 1656, the Spaniards chose the present-day location of Mission San Luis to build their fort. This area is on a hilltop and has a clear view of the land below. "The area reminds me of our family's farm in Puerto Rico," said Grace's mother. "Oh yeah...It's also on a hilltop!" remembers Grace. It was very important that their fort be on a hilltop, because the Spaniards needed to be able to see if anyone was coming to attack them.

Today, visitors to Mission San Luis can experience what is was like to live among the Apalachee and the Spaniards. "This place is amazing," says Grace. As Grace walks to the central area known as the plaza, she says, "I bet this is where they held special ceremonies and played games." The church and the Apalachee chief's house are just a few of the many buildings that have been rebuilt to look the way they did hundreds of years ago. Grace also enjoys looking at all of the artifacts from Spanish households. The past really does come alive at Mission San Luis!

The tour guides and others who work at Mission San Luis enjoy helping visitors learn about the past.

Think About It Based on this story, why do you think it is important to visit places like Mission San Luis? As you read the chapter ahead, think about how learning about the past affects your life today.

Lesson 1

America's First Peoples

Envision It!

Look at the picture. Write what natural resource was used to build these homes.

Every community has a history shaped by the people who first lived there. Your community is special because of its past as well as its present.

Native American Groups

KEY
— Present-day border

ARCTIC

SUBARCTIC

PACIFIC NORTHWEST

PLATEAU

PACIFIC OCEAN

CALIFORNIA

GREAT BASIN

PLAINS

NORTHEAST WOODLANDS

SOUTHEAST WOODLANDS

ATLANTIC OCEAN

SOUTHWEST

Gulf of Mexico

0 — 1,000 mi
0 — 1,000 km

N W E S

Cultural Groups

Native Americans were the first people to settle in North America. There were many different Native American groups and they each had their own cultures and **customs,** or special ways of doing things.

The map shows the regions of North America where Native Americans lived. Each group used the natural resources in their region to meet their needs. Native Americans who lived in the Pacific Northwest caught fish from the Pacific Ocean. Those living on the Plains used the rich soil there for farming.

1. **Underline** two ways Native Americans used natural resources to live.

Vocabulary

custom   reservation
longhouse   government
confederacy   tradition
cooperate

Cherokee of the Southeast

Long ago, the Native American group called the Cherokee settled in the forests of the southeastern United States. The Cherokee settled in this area because of geography: rich soil, rivers, and trees.

The Cherokee first settled in North America more than 1,000 years ago. They were hunters and farmers. They ate meat, fruit, and vegetables. They used trees to build houses. They covered the wooden frames with mud from the nearby riverbanks. Later, the Cherokee built log homes that kept out the cold and snow in winter.

A famous Cherokee named Sequoyah (sih KWOI uh) invented a system for writing the Cherokee language. Once people learned the 86 symbols, they could read and write the language.

2. ◎ **Main Idea and Details Describe** how the Cherokee used natural resources.

....

....

....

The Cherokee used natural resources to make pottery and to weave baskets.

Iroquois of the Northeast

The Iroquois settled in the forests of what is now central and northern New York and southern Canada. Like the Cherokee, the Iroquois chose this area to settle because of geography. The forests had plenty of animals and plants. The Iroquois used rivers for fishing and traveling.

Like the Cherokee, the Iroquois used trees to build their houses. However, Iroquois houses had a different shape than Cherokee houses. They were up to 200 feet long! Since these homes were longer than they were wide, they were called **longhouses.** Longhouses could be home to as many as ten families. Each family had its own living space. Fires were built down the middle of the longhouse, and families on each side shared a fire.

More than 500 years ago, the Iroquois formed a confederacy. A **confederacy** is a formal agreement, or treaty, between groups to work together. The Iroquois Confederacy had five groups; the Mohawk, Oneida, Onondaga, Cayuga, and Seneca peoples all shared a similar culture. The Confederacy was also called the Five Nations. It had rules to protect the rights of each of the five groups. Each group voted on important Iroquois decisions.

3. List three features of longhouses.

....

....

....

An Iroquois village

Hiawatha was an Onondaga chief and a member of the Iroquois Confederacy.

Group Cooperation

As the Iroquois Confederacy shows, some Native Americans groups **cooperated**, or worked together. Even though the Confederacy allowed each group to rule itself, the Five Nations felt it was best to come together so they could be stronger and more powerful. The main purpose of the Iroquois Confederacy was the *Great Law of Peace*. This law said that all decision making had to be done peacefully. No one was allowed to hurt anyone if groups disagreed.

Native American groups not only worked with one another, but they also cooperated with the first settlers from England. When these settlers came about 300 years ago, some Native Americans taught them how to plant crops such as pumpkin, squash, beans, and corn. They also taught settlers different ways to fish in the shallow water.

At times, however, Native American groups went to war against each other. About 400 years ago, the Iroquois fought wars against the Huron, Erie, and Algonquin groups. The Iroquois had traded beaver furs with European settlers for guns and other supplies. When the beaver population began to die out, the Iroquois traveled west into other Native American lands to look for beaver. Because the Iroquois had better weapons than the groups they were fighting against, they won what were called the Beaver Wars.

4. ◉ **Cause and Effect**
Underline the effects of the Iroquois groups working together.

Native Americans bring beaver furs to English settlers.

Native Americans Today

Today, there are about 2 million Native Americans living in the United States. About 1 million Native Americans live in Canada.

Some Native Americans in the United States live on **reservations**, or lands that the United States government set aside for them many years ago. Each reservation has its own **government**. A government is a system of ruling people. Native Americans who live on reservations have to obey the laws created by this government. They not only have to follow the laws set up by their reservation's government, but they also have to follow the laws made by the United States government.

Ben Nighthorse Campbell wears traditional Native American clothing to a United States government meeting.

Ben Nighthorse Campbell is part of the Northern Cheyenne group and serves as a member of the group's Council of Chiefs. He also served as a member of the United States government for 18 years.

Native Americans have traditions. A **tradition** is a special way that a group does something that is passed down over time. Some Cherokee traditions include games, dances, songs, and clothing. Some Native Americans wear traditional clothing, such as feathered headdresses. The photograph shows Ben Nighthorse Campbell wearing a headdress that stands for bravery and courage.

5. Look at the photo. **Describe** another part of Campbell's clothing that might have special meaning.

....

....

6. ◉ **Main Idea and Details Fill in** the chart with details that support the main idea.

Native Americans chose where to settle because of geography.

7. ? **Write** about traditions in your family or community that came from the past.

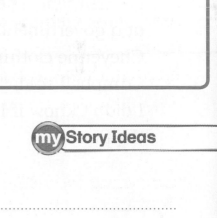
my Story Ideas

....

....

....

....

....

⬛ **Stop!** I need help with ....

⏸ **Wait!** I have a question about ....

▶ **Go!** Now I know ....

Sequence

Sequence is the order in which events take place. Words such as *first, second, third, then, after, next, finally, past, future, now,* and *later* can help you find the sequence of events. Dates can help you find the sequence of events, too. Look for days, months, and years.

Read below about Ben Nighthorse Campbell. Then read the chart that shows the sequence of events.

Ben Nighthorse Campbell was born in California in 1933. About 50 years later, he began working in the United States government. Then in 2004, Campbell arrived at a government meeting in his traditional Cheyenne clothing. During his speech, Campbell said, "It was a bit of a tight schedule. I didn't know if I could change before I got to the floor."

Ben Nighthorse Campbell

Ben Nighthorse Campbell

Ben Nighthorse Campbell was born in California in 1933.

About 50 years later, he began working in the United States government.

Then in 2004, Campbell arrived at a government meeting in his traditional Cheyenne clothing.

Read the passage about Sequoyah. Then **fill in** the sequence of events in the chart below. **Circle** the words or dates in the passage that helped you find the correct sequence.

Sequoyah made a very important contribution to Cherokee culture. In 1821, he developed a set of symbols to go with all 86 syllables of the Cherokee language. Then the language was taught in all Cherokee schools. Finally, the Cherokee began to print books and newspapers in the Cherokee language.

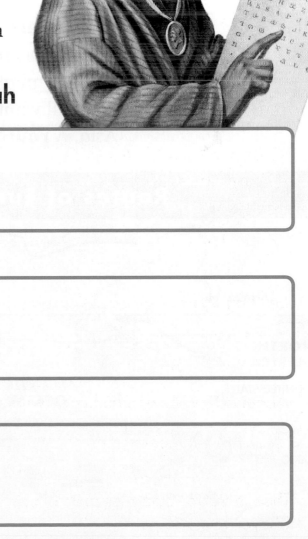

Sequoyah

Sequoyah

Early Explorers

Envision It!

Suppose you traveled to the place in the picture. Describe what you might find when you get there.

Do you like going to new places and meeting new people? An explorer does! An **explorer** is a person who travels looking for new lands and discoveries.

Explorers Sail From Europe

Explorers from Europe thought traveling to Asia by water might take less time than traveling by land. They all wanted to be the first to find a water route to Asia. A **route** is the course you take to get somewhere.

Routes of European Explorers

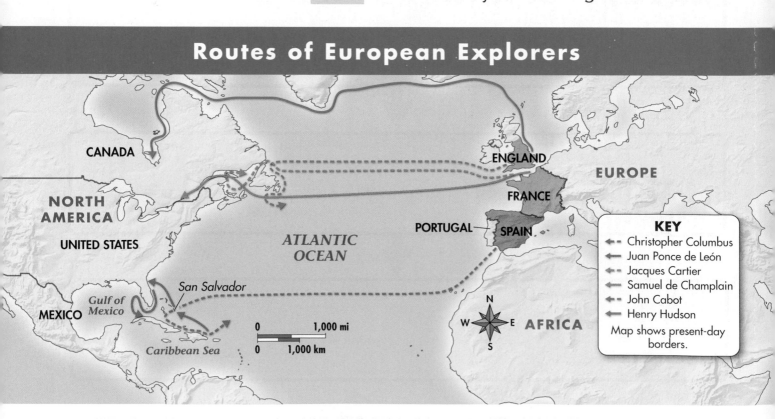

CANADA

ENGLAND

EUROPE

FRANCE

NORTH AMERICA

PORTUGAL — SPAIN

UNITED STATES

ATLANTIC OCEAN

San Salvador

Gulf of Mexico

MEXICO

Caribbean Sea

N W E S

AFRICA

0   1,000 mi
0   1,000 km

KEY
- Christopher Columbus
- Juan Ponce de León
- Jacques Cartier
- Samuel de Champlain
- John Cabot
- Henry Hudson

Map shows present-day borders.

Vocabulary

explorer
route

More than 500 years ago, in the 1480s, explorers from Portugal began to search for a water route to Asia by sailing east around Africa. In the early 1490s, Spain was the first country to send explorers west across the Atlantic Ocean. These explorers were looking not only for a way to travel to Asia by water, but also for spices and herbs needed for cooking and medicine. In addition, they hoped to find gold, silk, and other riches.

By the late 1490s, English explorers were also trying to find a water route to Asia. The English explorers wanted to own land in the Americas, so they sent explorers there, too.

By the early 1500s, France was also searching for a water route to Asia. During the search, French explorers built settlements and traded with Native Americans in what is now Canada.

1. ◎ **Sequence** **List** the countries in Europe in the order that they began searching for a water route to Asia.

....

....

Spices, gold, silk, gems

Spanish Explorers

Long ago, spices were very valuable. People used spices to keep food from spoiling. Spain hired Christopher Columbus, an explorer born in Italy, to sail to China to search for spices.

Columbus began his trip to China in 1492. He thought he could reach China by sailing west from Spain. He did not find China. He landed on an island off the coast of present-day Florida instead. When he first saw the people living there, he called them "Indians." That is because he thought he had reached the East Indies near southern China. Next, Columbus sailed to more islands. He set up a settlement on an island called Hispaniola (hihs pun YOH luh).

A group called the Taino (TYE noh) already lived on the island of Hispaniola. Their lives changed after the Spaniards, or people from Spain, arrived. Many Taino people died of diseases brought by the Spaniards.

Amerigo Vespucci was another explorer who sailed for Spain. He explored many places, including what is known today as Venezuela. North and South America were named in his honor.

Columbus had three ships: the Niña, the Pinta, and the Santa Maria.

French Explorers

After the French arrived in North America in the 1520s, they began to explore the land. They traveled north by river through the center of North America. Jacques Cartier sailed the St. Lawrence River in 1535.

Samuel de Champlain explored the St. Lawrence region and the Great Lakes. He founded Quebec City in 1608. Champlain learned a lot from the Native Americans and formed good relationships with them.

In 1634, Jean Nicolet tried to find the Northwest Passage to India, a water route that would link the Atlantic and Pacific oceans. He did not find it, but he explored Lake Michigan. Robert de La Salle explored the Great Lakes and the Mississippi River. In 1682, he claimed the entire Mississippi region for France.

2. List one area that Robert de La Salle explored.

....

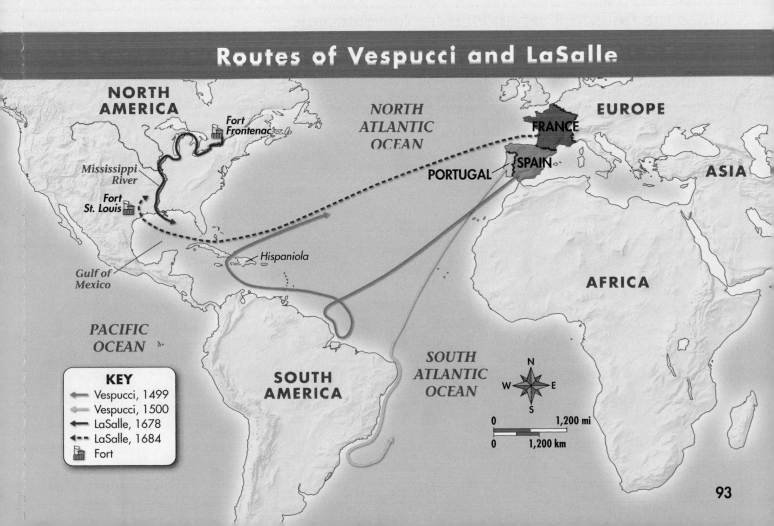

Routes of Vespucci and LaSalle

NORTH AMERICA

Fort Frontenac

Mississippi River

Fort St. Louis

Gulf of Mexico

PACIFIC OCEAN

NORTH ATLANTIC OCEAN

FRANCE

SPAIN

PORTUGAL

Hispaniola

EUROPE

ASIA

AFRICA

SOUTH AMERICA

SOUTH ATLANTIC OCEAN

N
W   E
S

KEY
- Vespucci, 1499
- Vespucci, 1500
- LaSalle, 1678
- LaSalle, 1684
- Fort

0   1,200 mi
0   1,200 km

English Explorers

English explorers wanted to explore the Americas, too. In June 1497, John Cabot arrived on the coast of North America and went on shore. Cabot explored the coast before sailing back to England. He wanted to tell everyone about his discovery. Later, England claimed all of North America. The English believed that Cabot had been the first person to discover this land.

In 1580, Sir Francis Drake became the first English explorer to sail around the world. He claimed land near present-day San Francisco for England. When Drake finished his trip, he was honored by the queen.

Beginning in 1607, Henry Hudson sailed for England to search for the Northwest Passage to India. After many failed attempts to do so, he moved to Holland. In 1609, he sailed from Holland, again trying to find the Northwest Passage. He could not find it, but he did discover a huge river in North America. The river is called the Hudson River and it is in New York state.

3. Underline the sentences that tell what each explorer helped to claim or discover.

Henry Hudson and his crew sail into the Hudson River.

4. ⊙ **Sequence Read** the list of events. Then **fill in** the chart by placing the events in the correct order.

1608 Samuel de Champlain founds Quebec City.
1634 Jean Nicolet explores Lake Michigan.
1609 Henry Hudson discovers the Hudson River.

Date	Event

5. ② **Choose** one explorer from this lesson. **Describe** his contribution to the region that he explored.

my Story Ideas

....

....

....

▢ **Stop!** I need help with ....

▯▯ **Wait!** I have a question about ....

▷ **Go!** Now I know ....

Timelines

A timeline shows when events took place. A timeline can be divided into years, decades, or centuries. A decade is ten years, and a century is 100 years. The timeline below shows when some states became part of the United States. It is divided by 50 years, or five decades.

Events are placed on a timeline in the order in which they happened. The event that happened first, or earliest, is placed on the left part of the timeline. Which of the four states shown below became a state first? If you look toward the left, you see that Virginia was the first to become a state. As you read the timeline from left to right, you learn which events happened first, second, third, and then last. The last, or most recent, event is shown on the right.

States Become Part of the Country

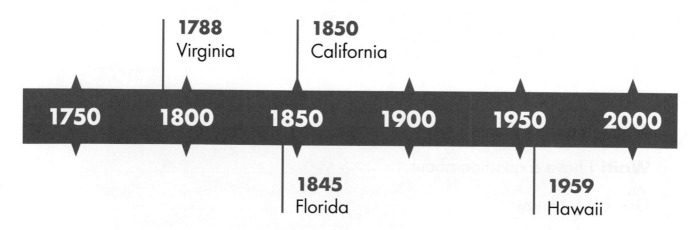

Look at the timeline. Which became a state first: California or Florida? If you read from left to right, you can see that Florida became a state before California. How many years apart did Florida and California become states? That's right! The answer is five years.

Try it!

Use the timeline to answer the questions below.

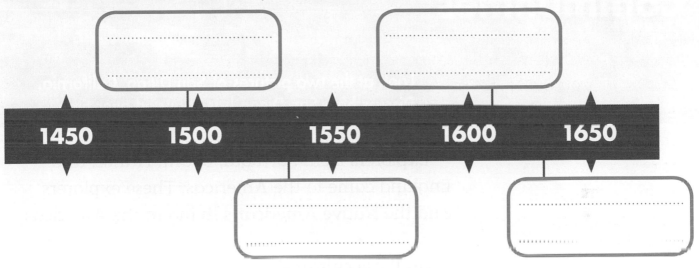

1. **Read** the list of years and events below. Then **fill in** the timeline with each explorer's name to show when he traveled.

   1535 Jacques Cartier sailed the St. Lawrence River.

   1492 Christopher Columbus sailed to the Americas.

   1634 Jean Nicolet explored Lake Michigan.

   1609 Henry Hudson discovered the Hudson River.

2. **Write** which explorer traveled first.

   ....

3. St. Augustine, Florida, was settled in 1565. **Write** if this happened before or after Jacques Cartier sailed the St. Lawrence River.

   ....

4. **List** which two explorers traveled within 25 years of each other.

   ....

   ....

Early Spanish Communities

Envision It!

Look at the two pictures of San Diego, California. Discuss how San Diego has changed over time.

Explorers from Portugal, Spain, France, and England came to the Americas. These explorers and the Native Americans living in the Americas had different cultures. Today, America is a rich mix of all these cultures.

Let's look more closely at the Spanish explorers who brought their culture to America.

Spanish Exploration in Florida

Some explorers who sailed to the Americas wanted gold, gems, and riches. Other explorers wanted to be famous.

Native Americans told a special **legend**, or a story from the past whose facts cannot be checked. The legend was about a magical spring whose water made people young again. Spanish explorer Juan Ponce de León wanted to find the spring. He wanted to find the Fountain of Youth.

In 1513, Ponce de León landed near present-day St. Augustine, Florida, during his search. He took control of the land for Spain. He named the land *La Florida*, which means "land of flowers."

Ponce de León

UNLOCK THE BIG ?

I will know about early Spanish explorers and settlers in North America.

Vocabulary

legend   colonize
fort   mission
colony   citizen

Ponce de León and his men did not find the Fountain of Youth. Ponce de León was very disappointed and left Florida. He sailed to what is known today as Puerto Rico and then back to Spain.

Ponce de León sailed to the west coast of Florida in 1521. He brought with him about 200 settlers, 50 horses and other animals, as well as farm tools. When Ponce de León and his party landed, they went to battle with a group of Native Americans. Ponce de León was wounded, and he died soon after.

Ponce de León was the first European to explore the area of Florida that is near St. Augustine. This led to others exploring the area after him.

1. **Explain** why Ponce de León was disappointed after he first left Florida.

....

....

....

Present-day Florida

Alabama   Georgia
Tallahassee ★   Jacksonville
                St. Augustine
Gulf of Mexico

                Tampa

                        Miami

KEY
★ Capital city
• City
0   140 mi
0   140 km
N W E S

Trouble Between Spain and France

Spain and France both wanted to build a settlement in Florida. In 1564, the French set up a fort and a colony on the St. John's River. A **fort** is a strong building or area that can be defended against enemy attacks. A **colony** is a place ruled by another country. The French fort was named Fort Caroline.

Fort Caroline was close to where the Spaniards had first landed. The Spanish treasure ships sailed along the Florida coast past Fort Caroline on their way from South America to Spain. The French fort and settlement threatened the Spanish ships. King Philip II of Spain came up with a plan to keep his ships safe from enemy attacks. He sent Don Pedro Menéndez de Avilés [ah vee LAYS], a Spanish explorer, to set up and lead a Spanish colony in Florida. The king felt he could depend on Menéndez to protect the Spanish ships.

King Philip II of Spain wanted to protect Spanish treasure ships, like the one shown at left, that were threatened by Fort Caroline, shown below.

King Philip ordered Menéndez to explore and settle Florida. He also told Menéndez to drive out any settlers and pirates from other countries. A pirate is a person who robs ships or boats at sea.

Menéndez arrived in Florida in 1565. Menéndez, his soldiers, and the settlers built a fort. They named it Castillo de San Marcos. The area was protected from the ocean. It could be defended easily. Then Menéndez started a settlement. He called it St. Augustine.

Menéndez defeated the French at Fort Caroline. Then a hurricane off the Atlantic Ocean wrecked an entire French fleet of ships. As a result, Spain controlled the coast of Florida. More Spaniards came to settle in St. Augustine. It became the first permanent European settlement in North America.

Don Pedro
Menéndez de Avilés

2. ⊙ **Sequence** **List** the sequence of events that led to the Spaniards settling St. Augustine.

....

....

....

....

St. Augustine is the oldest European city in the United States.

Spanish Settlements in California

After the Spaniards settled St. Augustine and other areas of Florida, they colonized other places. To **colonize** means to settle lands for another country. The Spaniards colonized parts of California. Here the Spaniards began towns called pueblos. They also built presidios, or forts. In California, just as in Florida, the Spaniards also set up missions. A **mission** is a settlement that has a church where religion is taught.

The first missions in California were built in the 1760s. They were set up as places to teach the Native Americans who lived there about Spanish culture and religion. Spain's king sent a religious leader named Junípero Serra to continue setting up missions. He and other leaders taught some of the Native Americans how to read and write, and how to prepare Spanish foods.

The Spaniards built pueblos like this one in present-day California.

Spain Loses Power

The country of Spain sent money to support the missions. Then, in the early 1800s, Spain told the religious leaders to stop building missions in California. The last mission was built in 1823.

People moving to California at that time wanted the Mexican government to make the Native Americans leave the missions. Mexico had control of California. So, in 1826, the head of government in California allowed many of these Native Americans to leave and become Mexican citizens. A **citizen** is an official member of a community. When they left the missions, the Native Americans needed new places to live and new jobs. Leaving the missions made their lives much more difficult.

3. ◉ **Sequence Underline** the sentences that tell when the first and last missions were built.

102

4. ⊙ **Summarize Write** two sentences telling what you learned about Spanish settlements in the Americas.

....

....

....

....

5. ⑦ **Describe** something unique about an early Spanish community.

....

....

....

⬛ **Stop!** I need help with ....

⏸ **Wait!** I have a question about ....

▶ **Go!** Now I know ....

Early French Communities

Envision It!

Write two things you see in this picture that tell you it shows a scene from the past.

French explorers traveled to many different parts of North America. The explorers brought French culture with them to the places they traveled. Many cities in North America founded by the French have kept parts of French culture.

The French Come to North America

In 1498, Vasco de Gama, an explorer from Portugal, found an all-water route to India. The French thought it might be faster to travel by inland waterways, so they explored rivers and streams.

In 1534, Jacques Cartier landed in Newfoundland. Then he explored the Gulf of St. Lawrence in present-day Canada. Cartier later sailed up the St. Lawrence River. He realized that it was not the direct route to Asia that he was looking for. Rough waters made traveling west too dangerous, so he returned home.

St. Louis, Missouri, is a city that was first settled by the French. In 1700, priests built a mission there. Native Americans joined the priests, but the settlement did not last.

Newfoundland, Canada

N
W E
S

0   300 mi
0   300 km

KEY
— Present-day border

ATLANTIC OCEAN

Quebec   Churchill River   Labrador

Newfoundland

Gulf of St. Lawrence

UNLOCK
THE BIG
?

I will know about early French explorers and settlers in North America.

Vocabulary

expedition
territory

Around 1760, a Frenchman named Pierre Laclede traveled to the same place the mission had been set up in 1700. Here he set up a trading post where things such as fur could be traded for other items. Laclede wanted to buy fur from the Native Americans. He named the area St. Louis for King Louis of France. Laclede said he wanted to set up "one of the finest cities in America." He did!

In time, France lost control of St. Louis. The city opened to new settlers and new businesses. However, French culture is still important in St. Louis today.

1. **Explain** why Cartier returned home instead of continuing his search for a direct route to China.

....

....

....

....

THE HISTORIC RIVERFRONT

LACLEDE'S LANDING

IN OLD SAINT LOUIS

The riverfront area of St. Louis is named in honor of Pierre Laclede.

Champlain Builds Quebec City

In 1608, Samuel de Champlain sailed from France to present-day Canada. He built a village near an area where a Native American group called the Huron already lived. He became friends with these Native Americans.

Champlain called his village Quebec City. England and France fought over this village. They both wanted to take control because of its location. Quebec City was on two waterways, the St. Lawrence and the St. Charles rivers. Settlers could use these rivers for trade and for traveling from one place to another. In 1759, the English won a battle against the French. As a result, French rule in Canada ended.

Today, French culture is still strong in Quebec City. People speak French, and they celebrate French customs and traditions. Old Quebec is a popular place to visit. It is the part of the city on top of a hill. Le Chateau (sha TOH) Frontenac is in the center of Old Quebec. It was built in 1893 on a hilltop overlooking the St. Lawrence River. Standing there, you can see for miles.

Le Chateau Frontenac

2. **Explain** why the location of Quebec City was so important.

....

....

....

....

....

....

Exploring the Mississippi River

The French explored inland waterways instead of traveling along the coast. In 1672, a Frenchman named Louis Joliet was put in charge of an expedition down the Mississippi River. An **expedition** is a trip made for a special reason. Joliet and a priest named Father Marquette traveled from present-day Canada down the Mississippi River. They traveled to the places that we know today as Green Bay, Wisconsin, and Chicago, Illinois. They learned that the Mississippi River empties into the Gulf of Mexico.

Earlier in the 1600s, Robert de La Salle explored the Great Lakes, the Mississippi River, and more. He claimed the entire Mississippi region for France. In 1634, Jean Nicolet took seven Native Americans with him in a large canoe and they went on an expedition to Lake Michigan. Nicolet also discovered what is now the state of Wisconsin.

Because of these explorers and others like them, the French began to gain power and control in North America. They claimed big parts of the continent for France.

3. ◎ **Sequence Write** who explored the Mississippi River first: Louis Joliet or Robert de La Salle.

....

Joliet traveled by canoe through the wild rapids near Montreal, Canada.

French Lose Power in North America

Both the British and the French wanted to control the northern part of North America. As a result, the French and Indian War began. It lasted from 1754 to 1763. Some Native Americans fought with the French against the British. The French lost the war and lost control of much of their land to the British.

In 1803, France continued to lose power in North America. The United States bought the Louisiana Territory from France. A **territory** is an area of land owned by a country either within or outside the country's borders. This is called the Louisiana Purchase. It stretched all the way from the Mississippi River to the Rocky Mountains and more than doubled the size of the United States.

A British soldier fighting in the French and Indian War

4. **Trace** the outline of the Louisiana Purchase. Then **draw** a dotted line around all of the states.

Louisiana Purchase

New Hampshire
Vermont
Mass.
New York
Rhode Island
Pennsylvania
Connecticut
New Jersey
Delaware
Maryland
Virginia
Ohio
Indiana Territory
Louisiana Purchase
ROCKY MOUNTAINS
Mississippi River
Kentucky
Tennessee
North Carolina
South Carolina
Georgia
Unorganized Territory
Mississippi Territory
ATLANTIC OCEAN

KEY
- State
- Territory
- Louisiana Purchase
- Disputed area

N W E S

0   400 mi
0   400 km

5. ⊙ **Sequence Write** three main events of the lesson in order from first to last. For each event, **explain** why it was important.


```
┌─────────────────────────────────────────┐
│                                           │
│                                           │
│                                           │
└─────────────────────────────────────────┘
                    │
                    ▼
┌─────────────────────────────────────────┐
│                                           │
│                                           │
│                                           │
└─────────────────────────────────────────┘
                    │
                    ▼
┌─────────────────────────────────────────┐
│                                           │
│                                           │
│                                           │
└─────────────────────────────────────────┘
```

6. ❓ **Describe** something unique about early French exploration.

my **Story Ideas**

....

....

....

⏹ **Stop!** I need help with ....

⏸ **Wait!** I have a question about ....

▶ **Go!** Now I know ....

Early English Communities

Envision It!

You are traveling by ship from England to Virginia in 1607. Draw three things you bring with you.

The exploration of North America opened up new lands to settle. The Spaniards and French started new settlements here. Now the English came, too.

Roanoke Colony

In 1587, Sir Walter Raleigh sent English settlers to start a colony in Roanoke Island in present-day North Carolina. Raleigh put John White in charge of the settlers. When Roanoke Island needed supplies, White sailed back to England, and he did not come back to the colony until 1590.

When John White returned to the island, all 113 men, women, and children he had left there were gone. White found the word *CROATOAN* carved on a tree. Some people think White told the settlers to carve this word if they moved while he was gone.

The lost colony is still a mystery. Some scientists believe there was a **drought**, or not enough water at that time. Some historians think the settlers may have gone to live with Native Americans, or that the settlers may have died from disease or hunger.

1. **Underline** the clue that tells what might have happened to the settlers of Roanoke Colony.

Roanoke Colony

UNLOCK THE BIG ? I will know why settlers came from England to North America.

Vocabulary

drought   Quaker
debt   pilgrim
interpreter

Jamestown

Around May 14, 1607, 105 English settlers arrived in what is now Virginia. Captain Christopher Newport brought them there on three ships: the *Godspeed*, the *Discovery*, and the *Susan Constant*. The settlers named their new colony Jamestown, and they named the nearby river after King James I.

Long before the English came, Native Americans built villages and planted crops in Virginia. Soon after the English settlers arrived, the settlers ran out of food. While Captain John Smith, a colony leader, searched for more food, Native Americans captured him and his group. They brought the group to their chief, Powhatan. One legend says Smith's life was saved by Powhatan's daughter, Pocahontas.

By the time Smith returned to Jamestown, only about 38 settlers were still alive. The rest had died of hunger and disease.

Pocahontas saves Captain John Smith.

2. **Explain** what Native Americans did long before the English came to Virginia.

....

....

England's Colonies

Everyone vanished at Roanoke Colony. Many died at Jamestown, yet the English settlers did not give up. In fact, they would go on to settle 13 colonies. By the 1660s, some settlers had moved south from Virginia. A colony was set up in present-day North and South Carolina. People called it Carolina.

The colonists who settled in the southern colonies brought African slaves with them. The enslaved Africans farmed the land.

In 1733, James Oglethorpe founded the Georgia colony. Oglethorpe set up this colony to help people who were in prison for not paying a debt. A **debt** is money that is owed to another person. People owing debts settled in Georgia. Oglethorpe wanted to give these people a chance to start a new life in his colony.

Mary Musgrove also played a key role in the founding of Georgia. Musgrove, a Creek Native American, served as an interpreter for Oglethorpe. As an **interpreter,** she helped the English and Native Americans speak with each other because she was able to speak both languages. She helped the Native Americans and English get along and keep the peace.

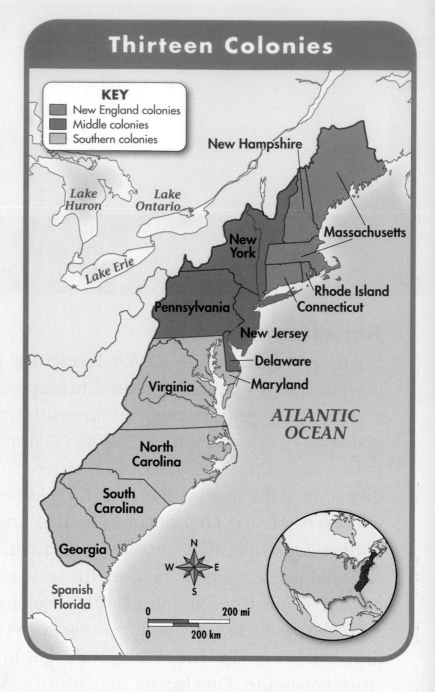

Thirteen Colonies

KEY
New England colonies
Middle colonies
Southern colonies

New Hampshire
Lake Huron
Lake Ontario
New York
Massachusetts
Lake Erie
Rhode Island
Connecticut
Pennsylvania
New Jersey
Delaware
Virginia
Maryland
ATLANTIC OCEAN
North Carolina
South Carolina
Georgia
Spanish Florida

N W E S

0   200 mi
0   200 km

3. Circle the names of the southern colonies on the map.

Settling the Middle Colonies

New York, New Jersey, Pennsylvania, and Delaware are the middle colonies. Can you guess how they got this name? They are right between the southern colonies and the colonies to the north.

In 1664, Holland lost the land that would later become three of the middle colonies in a war against the English. The Duke of York got one part of the land. He named it New York, after himself. The duke gave the other part of his land to two friends. These other parts eventually became the colonies of New Jersey and Delaware. Pennsylvania, however, was started in a very different way.

A statue of William Penn

William Penn started the colony of Pennsylvania as a "holy experiment." Penn was a Quaker. A **Quaker** is a follower of a religion that believes in peace and equal treatment for all people. Many people came to Penn's colony. People from Germany and Ireland were among the first settlers to come there for religious freedom.

Benjamin Franklin is one of the most famous people who lived in Philadelphia, Pennsylvania. He moved there because there were many more opportunities than in his home city of Boston, Massachusetts. Wherever Franklin went, he tried to make it a better place to live. He began Philadelphia's first fire department. Thanks to Franklin, Philadelphia became a safer city.

4. **Choose** one of the middle colonies, and **explain** how it was started.

....

....

....

Benjamin Franklin was a firefighter in Philadelphia.

New England Colonies

Massachusetts, Connecticut, Rhode Island, and New Hampshire were called the New England colonies.

In 1620, William Bradford led a group of Pilgrims on board a ship called the *Mayflower*. A **pilgrim** is a person who travels for a religious reason. Sixty-six days later, they landed in Provincetown Harbor in present-day Massachusetts. They came to the colonies to be free to follow their religion.

First, the Pilgrims formed a community in Plymouth, Massachusetts. Then, they wrote a plan of government called the Mayflower Compact. It said the colonists themselves would make laws for the good of the community. Everyone agreed to obey these laws. This was the first time European colonists in America had made laws for themselves.

People act out the first Thanksgiving.

Bradford became the leader. He was a good leader. The Pilgrims and Native Americans began trading food and other items. Squanto, a Native American who spoke English, served as an interpreter. In 1621, the Pilgrims and the Native Americans sat down to share in a harvest feast. Today, we mark this as the first Thanksgiving.

A woman named Anne Hutchinson did not follow the Pilgrims' beliefs. She began spreading her own beliefs. As a result, in 1634, she was forced to leave Massachusetts. She later founded Portsmouth, Rhode Island.

5. ⊙ **Sequence Underline** the first and second things the Pilgrims did when they came to America.

6. ⊙ **Main Idea and Details Fill in** the chart below with details that support the main idea.

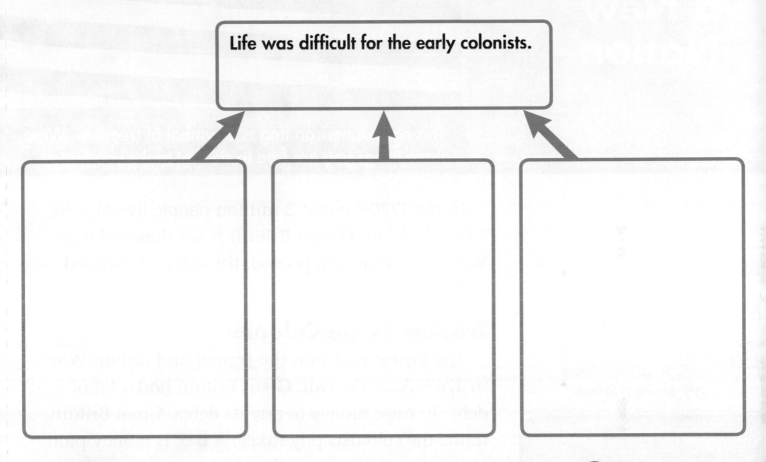

Life was difficult for the early colonists.

7. ❓ **Tell** one reason the English settled the Americas. **Write** why that reason is still important to us today.

 my Story Ideas

....

....

....

⬛ **Stop!** I need help with ....

⏸ **Wait!** I have a question about ....

▶ **Go!** Now I know ....

Creating a New Nation

Envision It!

This early American flag is a symbol of freedom. Write three things you are free to do that make you happy.

In the 1770s, about 2 million people lived in the 13 colonies, and Great Britain ruled these colonies. With each year that passed, the colonists wanted more and more to be free to rule themselves.

Trouble in the Colonies

The British had won the French and Indian War in 1763. After the war, Great Britain had a lot of debt. To raise money to pay its debts, Great Britain made the colonists pay taxes. A **tax** is money paid to a government. The colonists became extremely angry. They thought this was unfair because they did not have a say in the British government.

In 1764, the British passed the Sugar Act, which taxed most of the sugar brought into the colonies. Then in 1765, Great Britain passed the Stamp Act. The Stamp Act taxed all printed items, such as newspapers and legal papers.

The colonists became more angry, saying, "No taxation without representation!" They would not pay taxes unless they had a say in the government.

The Stamp Act ended, but there were new taxes on paper, glass, and lead. Many colonists refused to buy these things, so the British lost a lot of money.

American colonists were angry at Great Britain.

UNLOCK
THE BIG
?

I will know the causes and effects of the American Revolution.

Vocabulary

tax   independence
protest   revolution
legislature   constitution
patriot

In 1773, the British passed the Tea Act, which said the colonists could buy tea only from Great Britain. To **protest**, or complain, some colonists dressed as Native Americans. They went on British ships in Boston Harbor, and they dumped all the tea overboard! This was called the Boston Tea Party. The British were angry, so they closed Boston Harbor and also took many powers away from the Massachusetts legislature. A **legislature** is a part of government that makes laws.

The problem was over money, power, and control. Who should rule America: Great Britain or the colonists?

1. **Explain** why the colonists dumped all of the tea overboard in Boston Harbor.

....

....

....

....

The Boston Tea Party

American Patriots

Many American colonists known as Patriots grew more and more angry about British rule. A **patriot** is a person who loves and defends his or her country and upholds people's rights. The Patriots wanted the American colonies to be free.

The Patriots came from different backgrounds. Some were young, like Nathan Hale. Others were older, like Benjamin Franklin. Some were leaders, like Thomas Jefferson. Others were farmers, like Daniel Shays. They all worked hard to win **independence,** or freedom, for the colonies.

On April 18, 1775, a Patriot named Paul Revere rode from Boston to Lexington, Massachusetts, to warn colonial leaders Samuel Adams and John Hancock that British troops were coming to arrest them. Revere also wanted to stop the British from taking the colonists' weapons. He went to each house along his ride to warn everyone that the British were coming.

A war was about to begin. The War for Independence, or the war between the American colonies and the British, is also called the American Revolution. A **revolution** takes place when people want to take over the government that rules them and create a new one. The war started on April 19, 1775, in the towns of Lexington and Concord in Massachusetts.

Paul Revere's ride

2. Write why people became Patriots.

....

....

....

Freedom and Government

In the summer of 1776, Thomas Jefferson wrote the Declaration of Independence. It told the world why the colonies were breaking away from Great Britain. It explained what the new nation stood for.

The first part said that people have rights that the government must protect. The second part listed the complaints the colonists had against the British king. The third part said the colonies were now free and independent states and not part of Great Britain.

The American Revolution lasted eight years. It took America that long to win independence from Great Britain. Fifty-five people met in Philadelphia in May 1787 to write a new plan of government, the United States Constitution. A **constitution** is a written plan of government that explains the beliefs and laws of a country. George Washington, Benjamin Franklin, and James Madison were three well-known and respected leaders who helped write the Constitution.

On September 17, 1787, the members completed their work. They had written a new plan of government for the United States. The people, not a king, would rule the new, independent nation.

3. ◎ **Summarize List** three things that were included in the Declaration of Independence.

....

....

....

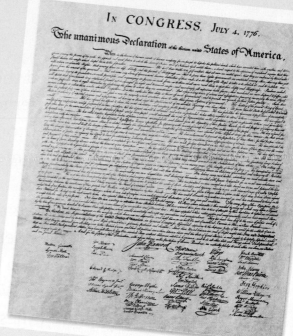

Declaration of Independence

Signing the Declaration of Independence

Washington, D.C.

George Washington led the colonial soldiers in the American Revolution. After the war, he wanted to go to his home at Mount Vernon, Virginia, and farm his land. Other leaders wanted Washington to lead the new government.

On February 4, 1789, the people elected Washington our first president. Lawmakers decided to build the new capital at a place they called Federal City. Today, it is known as Washington, D.C.

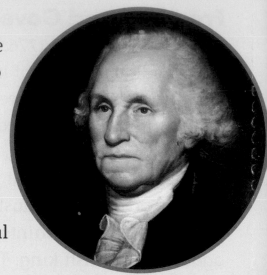

George Washington

One hundred square miles of land was set aside. An African American named Benjamin Banneker surveyed, or measured, the land to figure out its border. Banneker had taught himself to survey land by studying the stars in the night sky. He used stones to mark the land at each mile.

In 1791, a Frenchman named Pierre L'Enfant designed Washington, D.C. He chose the sites for the two most important buildings there: the Capitol Building and the White House. He also designed wide streets lined with trees. He set up spaces so that more statues could be built to honor important people.

Washington, D.C., is named after George Washington. He is remembered as a great leader. A general summed up George Washington's life this way: ". . . first in war, first in peace, and first in the hearts of his countrymen."

4. **Underline** the names of the people who helped create Washington, D.C.

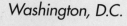

Washington, D.C.

5. ◉ **Sequence List** the events below in the order they happened.

> • The U.S. Constitution is completed.
> • Great Britain passes the Stamp Act.
> • The French and Indian War ends.
> • Paul Revere rides to Lexington.

1763 ....

....

1765 ....

....

1775 ....

....

1787 ....

....

6. ⓘ **Explain** how colonial leaders helped build a new nation.   🅜Ⓨ Story Ideas

....

....

....

....

....

⬛ **Stop!** I need help with ....

❚❚ **Wait!** I have a question about ....

▶ **Go!** Now I know ....

Review and Assessment

Lesson 1

America's First Peoples

1. **Fill in** the circle next to the correct answer.
   Why did the Iroquois settle in present-day New York state and Canada?
   - O to separate themselves from other groups
   - O to show they were strong leaders
   - O to use trees from the forests to build homes
   - O to look for beaver furs

Lesson 2

Early Explorers

2. **Fill in** the chart below with the correct information about each explorer.

Explorer	Country	Where They Explored
Christopher Columbus		
Samuel de Champlain		
Sir Francis Drake		

Lesson 3

Early Spanish Communities

3. Write three ways the Spaniards colonized.

....

....

....

....

4. Circle two places that the Spaniards colonized.

- California

- Canada

- Florida

- New York

Lesson 4

Early French Communities

5. Explain what Pierre Laclede did in the city of St. Louis.

....

....

....

....

Early English Communities

6. Fill in the chart with two people linked to each colony.

Jamestown	Georgia	Pennsylvania

Creating a New Nation

7. Explain why laws passed by the British, such as the Stamp Act, made the colonists angry.

....

....

....

....

8. ⊙ **Sequence Number** the following events in order.

_____ The American Revolution began.

_____ The Boston Tea Party took place.

_____ George Washington became our first president.

_____ James Madison helped write the United States Constitution.

Go online to write and illustrate your own **myStory Book** using the **myStory Ideas** from this chapter.

 How does our past affect our present?

In this chapter you have learned about how our history affects our life today. Explorers came from all over the world to America. We learned from these early explorers.

Think about your own life. **Write** about something you learned in your past that helps you today.

....

....

||||||||||||||||||||||||||||||||||||||||||||||||||||||||||||||||||||

....

Now **draw** a picture showing something you learned when you were younger that you do or use today.

While you're online, check out the **myStory Current Events** area where you can create your own book on a topic that's in the news.

U.S. Government

Why do we have government?

Think about why leaders make rules. Then **write** about why rules are important.

....

....

....

....

Many people celebrate our government on Independence Day.

George Washington
America's First President

my Story Video

You may know of a story about George Washington when he was a child. In the story, his father gave him a hatchet. A hatchet is a small ax used to chop wood. One day, George chopped down a cherry tree with his hatchet. George's father saw the cherry tree on the ground. Shocked, he asked his son, "What did you do?"

"I cannot tell a lie, Pa," George said. "I cut the tree down with my hatchet." Even though George's father was unhappy that George cut down the tree, he was happy that his son was honest.

Today, we know that this story is not true. It was likely made up to show that George Washington was an honest person. However, there are stories about him that are true. These stories are based on facts. Here are some facts about Washington.

In 1732, Washington was born in Virginia. He lived with his family on a farm. In 1743, Washington went to live with family at Mount Vernon. Soon after, he worked as a surveyor. As a surveyor, he measured and charted land.

Washington worked as a surveyor.

127

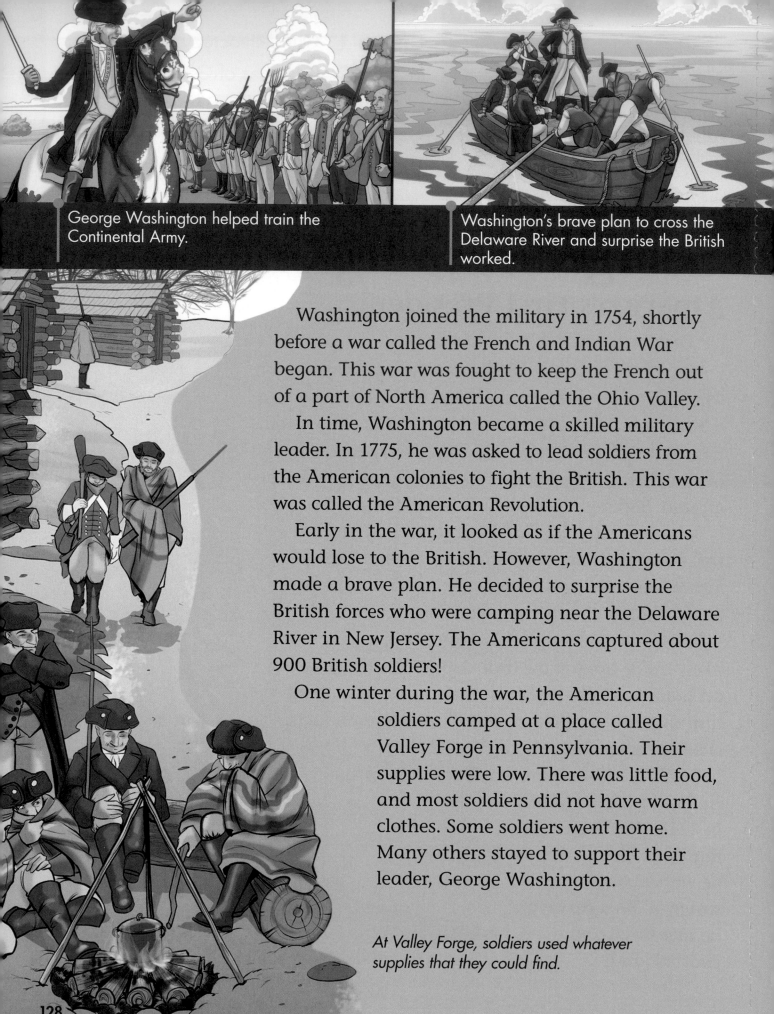

George Washington helped train the Continental Army.

Washington's brave plan to cross the Delaware River and surprise the British worked.

Washington joined the military in 1754, shortly before a war called the French and Indian War began. This war was fought to keep the French out of a part of North America called the Ohio Valley.

In time, Washington became a skilled military leader. In 1775, he was asked to lead soldiers from the American colonies to fight the British. This war was called the American Revolution.

Early in the war, it looked as if the Americans would lose to the British. However, Washington made a brave plan. He decided to surprise the British forces who were camping near the Delaware River in New Jersey. The Americans captured about 900 British soldiers!

One winter during the war, the American soldiers camped at a place called Valley Forge in Pennsylvania. Their supplies were low. There was little food, and most soldiers did not have warm clothes. Some soldiers went home. Many others stayed to support their leader, George Washington.

At Valley Forge, soldiers used whatever supplies that they could find.

Many Americans trusted Washington.

Washington and other leaders helped build a strong government.

The American Revolution ended in 1783. The American colonies won and were now free from Great Britain. The colonies became the United States of America. After the war, Washington planned to go home to Mount Vernon. However, he had become a well-known leader and had more work to do. In 1787, Washington traveled to a large meeting in Philadelphia called the Constitutional Convention. American leaders came together to write a plan for the new government. This plan became known as the United States Constitution.

In 1788, Washington was elected as the first president of the United States. He used the ideas and laws written in the Constitution to show what the job of the president should be. Today, presidents still do many of the same tasks that Washington did as president.

Washington died at Mount Vernon in 1799. The story of the cherry tree was not true. However, through his actions, we know that Washington was honest, brave, and loyal to his country.

Think About It Based on this story, how did Washington show he was loyal to his country? As you read the chapter ahead, think about what Washington's life shows you about supporting the government.

Our Democracy

Circle the pictures that show items that help keep people safe.

Think about some of the rules that you follow in your classroom. Some rules help keep order. For example, students should listen while others speak. Other rules keep everyone safe. During fire drills, it is important that everyone walk calmly and quietly. Students, teachers, and principals all make and follow rules to help schools run smoothly.

Why We Need Government

In communities all around the world, people set up governments. People need governments to make laws that keep order and help communities run smoothly. Just as there are classroom rules, there are laws that describe how citizens should behave. Some of these laws keep people safe. There are speed limits and traffic lights to help prevent automobile accidents. There are also laws that protect people's rights.

People also need governments to provide services that they cannot provide for themselves. Governments hire police officers and firefighters. Police officers make sure people follow laws. Like firefighters, they work to protect people and their property.

Firefighters protect people.

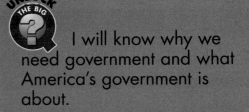

Vocabulary

democracy
represent
liberty

There are different forms, or types, of government in different communities around the world. The government of the United States is run by its citizens. It is a democracy. In a **democracy,** people vote to choose who leads the community, state, or nation. People may also vote on laws that everyone must follow.

In some governments around the world, the people do not have a say in who leads them. The country may be ruled by a king or queen whose father or mother was the king or queen before them. A king or queen may or may not allow people to vote for laws. A country may also be ruled by a single person or a small group who rule with complete power. In these countries, people have no say in who leads or in what the laws will be.

1. **Underline** the reasons people need government. Then **write** the form of government of the United States.

....

Governments place signs near roads to remind drivers to drive carefully.

Freedom and Happiness

In the 1700s, King George III and the British government ruled the colonies in North America. Many people living in the colonies, including Patrick Henry, spoke out against British rule. Henry and other colonists wanted people to **represent**, or speak for, them in government. They also wanted a government that protected the rights of all of its people, not just those in Great Britain. The rights that colonists wanted included the right to live freely, the right to follow any religion, the right to vote, and the right to a fair trial.

The colonists wanted **liberty**, or freedom, from British rule. They asked Thomas Jefferson to write the Declaration of Independence to tell the rights people should have.

"We hold these truths to be self-evident [clear], that all men are created equal, that they are endowed [born with] by their Creator with certain unalienable [secure] Rights, that among these are Life, Liberty and the pursuit of Happiness."

— Declaration of Independence

Patrick Henry speaks out against British rule.

The Declaration of Independence also stated that a government must protect citizens' rights. If a government took away these rights, the people could change the government or form a new one. The colonists did not have these rights when Great Britain ruled them. They fought a war against Great Britain to win these rights. This war was called the American Revolution. The Americans won the war in 1783.

2. ◉ **Cause and Effect Fill in** the chart with the missing cause and effect.

The American Revolution

Cause	Effect
	The colonists wrote the Declaration of Independence
Colonists fought against Great Britain in the American Revolution.	

An Independence Day celebration

133

The States Come Together

Even before the American Revolution was over, the American colonies declared themselves states in a new nation. After the war, the states faced problems. People in the different states argued over money and land. In addition, the government could not set rules for trade between the states. The Americans needed a plan to bring the country together. As a result, leaders gathered to write the United States Constitution.

Some of the laws in the Constitution are based on ideas from the government used long ago in Greece. These ideas include that the government gets its power from the people. In the United States, people vote for leaders to represent them. In Greece, however, each citizen voted only on issues.

Before the Constitution could become law, nine of the 13 states had to sign it. In doing so, the states agreed that the Constitution was the highest law. Although each state had its own constitution and laws, state laws could not go against the United States Constitution.

The United States Constitution

Leaders met in Philadelphia to write the Constitution.

In 1788, New Hampshire was the ninth state to sign and agree to the U.S. Constitution. The U.S. Constitution then became the new plan of government.

3. ◉ **Summarize Write** a summary of how the United States Constitution changed the states.

....

....

....

Got it?

4. ◉ **Summarize Write** a summary about why people need government.

....

....

....

....

5. ❓ **Explain** why American leaders wrote the U.S. Constitution. my Story Ideas

....

....

....

⬛ **Stop!** I need help with ....

⏸ **Wait!** I have a question about ....

▶ **Go!** Now I know ....

Summarize

When you write a summary, you tell about the main idea and key details of a passage in your own words. To get ready to write a summary, first find the main idea of a passage. The main idea is the most important idea. Next, find the key details. Details give you facts about the main idea.

Now you are ready to write your summary! In the first sentence, put the main idea in your own words. Then write one or two sentences that describe the details. Again, use your own words.

Read the passage about the American flag. Notice the main idea and details. Then read the summary below.

The American Flag

We have rules about how to display the American flag because it is important to show respect for it. One rule is that when the flag is hung on a wall, the blue part with the stars must be on the top left as you face the flag. Many people hang the flag on a wall when they hang it inside of a building. Another rule is that the flag should never touch the floor or the ground.

> This sentence states the main idea.

> These sentences are the key details.

Summary

There are rules about showing the American flag. The flag should be hung a certain way on a wall. It should also stay above the ground.

> This sentence tells about the main idea in the writer's own words.

> These sentences tell about the key details in the writer's own words.

Read the paragraph below. Then **answer** the questions.

> You may have heard the saying that signing a paper is "putting your John Hancock" on it. This saying dates back to 1776 when the Declaration of Independence was written. A group of leaders met in Philadelphia to decide what should be included in the Declaration. After Thomas Jefferson finished writing it, the leaders signed the document before sending it to the British king. John Hancock was one of the first people to sign it. He signed his name very large so that the king would be able to read it without his glasses! As a result, Hancock's signature became very well-known. Now when people are asked to put their signature on something, the signature is known as their "John Hancock."

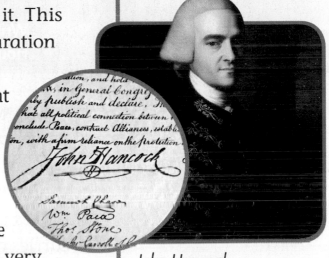

John Hancock

1. **Circle** the main idea.

2. **Underline** the key details that tell about the main idea.

3. **Write** a summary of the main idea and key details.

....

....

....

....

Branches of Government

Write who you think lives and works in the White House in Washington, D.C.

The writers of the U.S. Constitution wanted to make sure the power to rule the nation was divided equally. They organized the government into three parts, or branches. The **legislative** branch makes laws. The **executive** branch enforces, or carries out, the laws. The judges in the **judicial** branch make sure that laws are fair. Each branch has specific duties and responsibilities in our government. No one branch has more power than any other branch.

United States Capitol Building

The Legislative Branch

The legislative branch is called **Congress.** Congress has two parts: the Senate and the House of Representatives.

The Senate is made up of two representatives from each state. A **representative** is a person chosen to speak for others. Citizens vote to choose these representatives. There are 50 states. How many people serve in the Senate? There are 100 senators! Senators are elected every six years, and they can be elected many times.

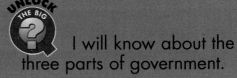
Vocabulary

legislative	representative
executive	bill
judicial	veto
Congress	Cabinet

The House of Representatives has many more representatives. There are 435! That is because the number of representatives in the House depends on each state's population, or the number of people living there. Alaska covers a large area, but it does not have a large population. Therefore, Alaska has only one representative. The state of Texas is large, and it has a large population. It has 32 representatives. All representatives are elected every two years. Like senators, these representatives speak for the people who vote for them.

The representatives in Congress make laws for the country. Some laws deal with safety while other laws make sure that all people are treated fairly. All laws begin as ideas. Once an idea is written down for the government to decide on, it is called a **bill**. Before a bill can become a law, both parts of Congress must vote on it and approve it. The bill is then sent to the president to sign.

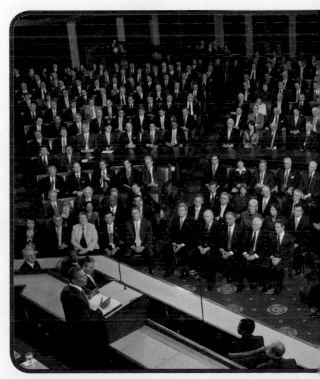

Congress meets in the U.S. Capitol.

1. **Underline** the job of Congress. **Circle** what happens to a bill after Congress approves it.

The Executive Branch

The executive branch carries out the laws. This branch is headed by the president of the United States. All the voters in the nation can elect the president. The president serves a term of four years and can only be elected for two terms. The president lives and works in the White House in Washington, D.C.

The president has more than one role in our government. One responsibility is to sign bills so they become laws. However, if the president does not agree with a bill, the president may **veto,** or reject, it. If a bill is vetoed, the only way it can become a law is if most of the members of Congress vote again to approve it.

The president is in charge of the United States military. This means the president is the commander-in-chief of soldiers in the Army, the Navy, the Marines, and the Air Force. The president also represents our country to the rest of the world. As a world leader, the president meets with leaders from other countries to work together to solve problems.

Mount Rushmore is in South Dakota. It shows the faces of Presidents Washington, Jefferson, Roosevelt, and Lincoln.

The president also works with the Cabinet. The **Cabinet** is a group of advisors, or people who tell a leader what they think about a subject. Each advisor leads one of the 15 different departments, or groups, in the executive branch. These advisors help provide the president with information about important issues in the country. These issues may be about education, health care, or security. The president selects these advisors. However, the Senate must approve the president's choices.

The president's office in the White House is called the Oval Office.

2. ◉ **Summarize Write** a summary of the president's responsibilities.

....

....

....

....

The Judicial Branch

The judicial branch of the government is made up of courts. Judges in the courts make sure that laws are fair. They also decide the consequences, or the results, for people who break laws.

The Supreme Court is the highest court in the United States. It has nine judges. Judges in the Supreme Court are called justices. The Supreme Court justices make sure the laws passed by Congress follow the U.S. Constitution. The justices also decide court cases between citizens of different states.

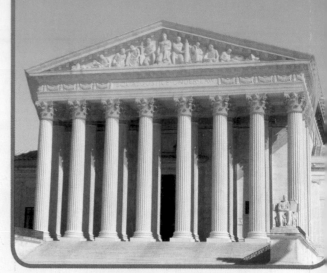

United States Supreme Court Building

The president nominates, or chooses, the justices for the Supreme Court. However, Congress must approve each choice. Supreme Court justices do not have a term limit. Once a person becomes a justice, he or she can serve for any amount of time.

The U.S. Constitution includes ways to make sure that the three branches of government work together. This system is called checks and balances. This means that each branch can check the actions of another. This helps make sure that the three branches share the power to rule. One branch does not have more power than the other branches.

The nine justices of the Supreme Court

3. Write two sentences to describe the roles of the justices who serve on the U.S. Supreme Court.

....

....

....

....

Got it?

4. ◉ **Main Idea and Details Fill in** the chart to show the key facts about the three branches of government.

Branches of Government

Legislative Branch	Executive Branch	Judicial Branch

5. ❓ **Explain** why we have three branches of government.

(my)Story Ideas

....

....

....

■ **Stop!** I need help with ....

❙❙ **Wait!** I have a question about ....

▶ **Go!** Now I know ....

Levels of Government

Envision It!

Write why schools are important to a community.

The mayor of Newark, New Jersey, marches in a community parade.

There are three different levels of government in our country: local, state, and national. Each level provides services to citizens. The local, state, and national governments are each divided into the same branches: the executive branch, the legislative branch, and the judicial branch.

Local Government

Local governments serve cities and towns. They can be organized in different ways. However, in most cities and towns, people elect a mayor or city manager as the head of the executive branch. A **mayor** is a leader of a community.

The people who make the rules and laws in a community are part of a city or town council. A **council** is a group that makes laws. Council members are often chosen by the people in a community. These lawmakers make up the legislative branch.

The judicial branch is made up of the city's or town's courts. A judge decides what happens to people who do not follow laws. Sometimes a jury, or group of citizens, decides if a person broke a law.

Vocabulary

mayor
council
governor
census

The local government provides many services that people use every day. It is in charge of the police department and the fire department. The local government also provides schools, libraries, and parks. It makes sure that trash is collected. It may also cut down trees that have been damaged in storms. The local government takes care of roads. It paves roads so they are smooth. It paints lines on roads and puts up signs so the roads are safe for drivers.

Where does the local government get the money to pay for all these services? Some money comes from the state government. Other services are paid for by the taxes that the local government collects. Sometimes citizens pay a fee to use services. For example, many large cities provide buses for transporting people in the city. However, people must pay to ride the bus.

1. ◉ **Main Idea and Details Underline** some of the services a local government provides.

Local governments make sure roads are clear of snow.

State Government

Each state has a state government that runs it. The states also have constitutions. State constitutions describe the responsibilities of the governor, the legislature, and the courts. The **governor** is the head of a state's executive branch and is elected by the people in the state.

The state legislature makes laws for the state. Nearly all 50 states divide the legislative branch into the Senate and the House of Representatives. The people in each state elect the members of their state legislature. These lawmakers meet in the capitol building in the state's capital city.

State governments also have courts in their judicial branch. Judges who work in state courts listen to issues that local courts could not solve.

The state government provides services, too. It decides the rules for voting, such as if a person must show identification. State governments also work with local governments to keep up state highways.

Before he became president, Jimmy Carter was governor of Georgia.

2. **Write** the name of your governor and your state capital.

....

....

....

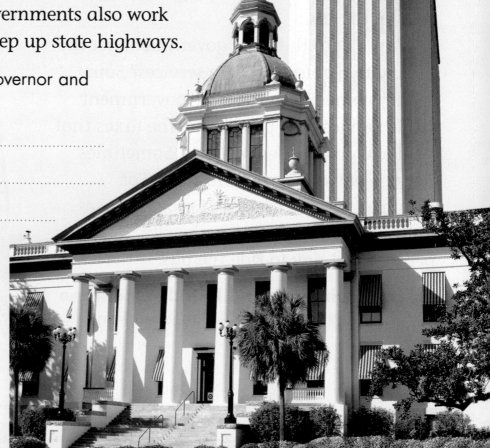

Members of the Florida legislature meet in this building in the capital city of Tallahassee.

National Government

The three branches of the national, or federal, government serve as a model for the other two levels of government in the United States. The president, members of Congress, and the Supreme Court justices share the responsibilities of running the country and serving all of the people.

The national government also provides services that are not given at the local and state level. The national government prints paper money and makes coins. It runs the United States Postal Service. It is in charge of trade between states and between countries. The national government also hires workers called rangers to manage the national parks.

The national government serves the whole nation in other ways, too. Every ten years the national government takes a **census**, or a count of the population. This count helps the government decide how much money different communities need. The national government can also organize an army. The army is used to protect the nation or its people. The government sometimes has soldiers provide services. Soldiers help people and communities after harsh storms.

Rangers teach about plants and animals in the national parks.

3. ◉ **Summarize** **Write** a summary of the services provided by the national government.

....

....

....

....

Governments Work Together

Even though the local, state, and national governments all have their own responsibilities, they often work together. They work together to complete large projects such as building roads, bridges, and buildings. Local and state leaders may also ask the national government for help if they are unable to provide enough help to their citizens.

The three levels of government do similar kinds of work. They all collect taxes from citizens. This money is used to pay for the services the governments provide. The national government collects taxes on the money people earn from their jobs. Some states also collect this tax. Local governments collect taxes on items people buy and on homes and businesses they own.

A local courtroom

The courts in all three levels also work together. If a local court does not resolve an issue, the case moves to a state court. Cases that are not resolved by state courts may then be decided by the United States Supreme Court justices.

4. ⊙ **Sequence Describe** what happens if a case is not decided in a local court.

....

....

....

....

....

5. ◉ **Main Idea and Details Fill in** the chart with three services provided by each of the three levels of government.

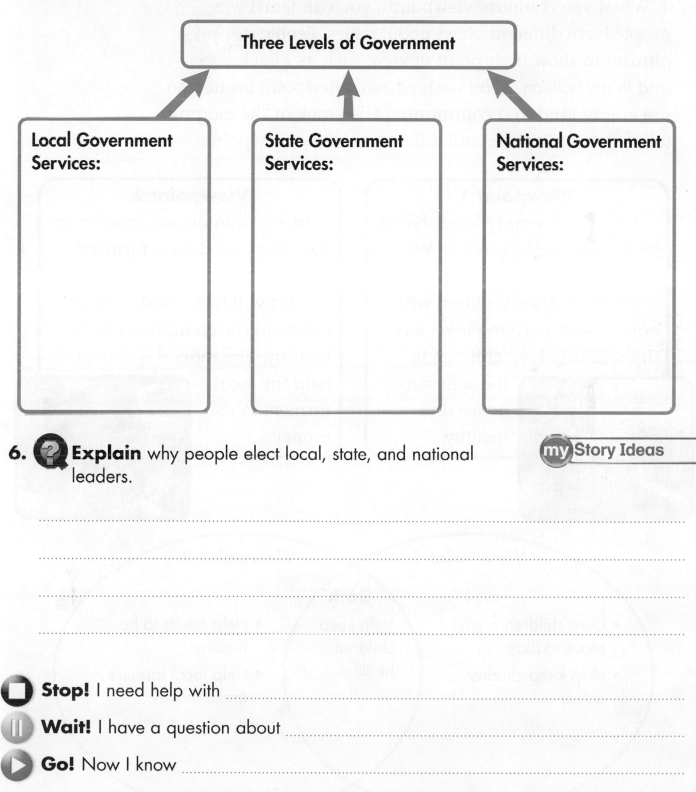

Three Levels of Government

Local Government Services:

State Government Services:

National Government Services:

6. ⍰ **Explain** why people elect local, state, and national leaders.

my **Story Ideas**

....

....

....

....

⏹ **Stop!** I need help with ....

⏸ **Wait!** I have a question about ....

▶ **Go!** Now I know ....

Compare Viewpoints

When you compare viewpoints, you can learn why people have different views about issues. People use key phrases to show their point of view, such as *I think*, *I feel*, and *in my opinion*. Read each citizen's viewpoint on how to use empty land in a community. Then look at the diagram to see the similarities and differences in the viewpoints.

Viewpoint 1

I think the empty land should be used for a playground. We should build a slide, swings, and a sandbox. Then children will have a safe place to play. I feel this will help keep children in the community active and healthy.

Viewpoint 2

In my opinion, we should use the empty land for a farmers' market. I think a farmers' market will help children and adults in the community to be healthy. The market will also help the local farmers make money.

Viewpoint 1

- Give children a safe place to play
- Help keep children active

Both

Help keep children healthy

Viewpoint 2

- Help adults to be healthy
- Help local farmers make money

Read each citizen's viewpoint about how to make a school less crowded. Then **fill in** the diagram to show the similarities and differences between the two viewpoints.

Viewpoint 1

Many new families have moved to our community. As a result, the school is very crowded because there are so many new students. I think we need to build a new school. It will cost money, but then classes will not be so crowded. Students will be able to have more time with their teachers.

Viewpoint 2

In my opinion, we should split the school schedule. Students in grades K–3 should go to school from 7:00 A.M. to 1:00 P.M. Students in grades 4–6 should go to school from 1:30 P.M. to 6:30 P.M. The school will be less crowded, and we will not have to pay to build a new school.

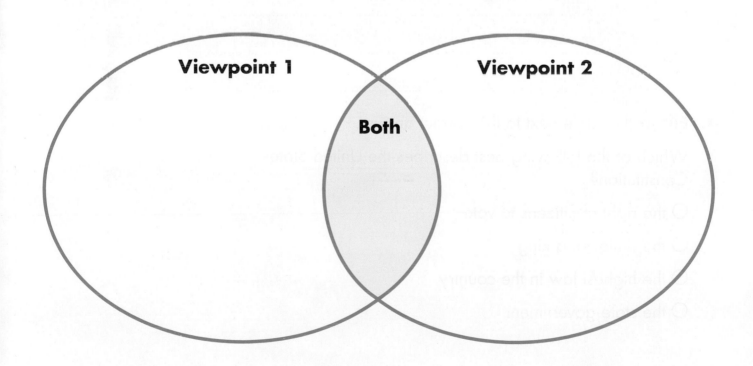

Review and Assessment

Lesson 1
Our Democracy

1. **Write** some of the ways that government helps keep us safe.

   ....

   ....

   ....

   ....

2. **Underline** the description of what it means to have liberty.

   to pay taxes   to go to school

   to work   to live freely

3. ◉ **Summarize Write** a summary about the rights that colonists believed all people should have.

   ....

   ....

   ....

   ....

4. **Fill in** the circle next to the correct answer.

   Which of the following best describes the United States Constitution?

   ○ the right of citizens to vote

   ○ the duties of a king

   ○ the highest law in the country

   ○ the state government

Review and Assessment

Lesson 2

Branches of Government

5. Draw a line to match each branch of government with its job.

executive branch   makes laws

legislative branch   makes sure laws are fair

judicial branch   carries out the laws

6. List the two parts of Congress.

....

....

7. Explain the different jobs the president has as the leader of the executive branch.

....

....

....

....

8. Circle the branch that includes the Supreme Court.

executive   legislative   judicial

9. Write the system that makes sure the three branches of government work together.

....

Lesson 3

Levels of Government

10. **Fill in** the circle next to the correct answer.

Which sentence describes a service the local government provides?

○ It prints money.

○ It manages national parks.

○ It runs the fire department.

○ It sets up the post office.

11. ◉ **Summarize Write** a summary about the services provided by state government.

....

....

....

....

12. **Underline** the leader of the national government.

mayor   governor   president

13. **Explain** how the three levels of government work together.

....

....

....

....

Go online to write and illustrate your own **myStory Book** using the **myStory Ideas** from this chapter.

Why do we have government?

The government keeps order, protects our communities, and provides us with many services. Each level of government, no matter what services it provides, works to help people.

Think about our government. **Explain** how your life might be different if our government were not a democracy.

....

....

....

....

Now **draw** a picture to show something you are free to do because our government makes it possible.

While you're online, check out the **myStory Current Events** area where you can create your own book on a topic that's in the news.

Citizenship

THE BIG ? How can I participate?

Describe some ways that people help others. Then write about a time when you did something to help someone else.

....

....

....

....

....

....

*Boys and Girls Clubs of America like this one provide
a place for young people to learn and have fun.*

Volunteering
Mentor, Tutor, Friend

my Story Video

Alicia is a teen volunteer at the Boys and Girls Club in her neighborhood. A volunteer is a person who improves the community and helps others. Today, Alicia is taking a 9-year-old girl named Kareena on a tour of the club. Kareena spends most days just like any other 9-year-old girl. She goes to school, helps with chores at home, and wonders what she will be when she grows up. Kareena is curious about what Alicia does as a volunteer at the Boys and Girls Club.

Alicia was eager to show Kareena the Boys and Girls Club.

"Hi Kareena, welcome to the Boys and Girls Club," says Alicia. "Let me show you around!" As Alicia and Kareena walk together through the club, Kareena is excited to see all of the great things it has: a game room, a study lounge, a computer room, an art room, and even a TV room. "Coming to a club like this would be fun," says Kareena. "Do you have checkers? I haven't played that since I was six!"

Alicia enjoys working at the front desk where she greets children as they arrive at the club.

Alicia likes helping children with their homework.

Alicia helps Kareena work on the computer.

For the past year, Alicia has volunteered at the Boys and Girls Club five days a week. Her favorite job is working at the front desk. As children arrive at the club, she checks them in and helps them decide what to do first. She also likes to help the younger children with their homework. Sometimes she gets to be creative and decorate the bulletin boards. "Even playing a simple board game can be a lot of fun with these kids," Alicia tells us.

Alicia went to the Boys and Girls Club as she was growing up and realized how important the volunteers were. Having a teenage mentor at the club had a big impact on Alicia. A mentor is someone you can trust to be loyal and helpful to you. "I want to be a role model," Alicia says, "and I want to help my community the way it helped me." Alicia enjoyed going to the club as a child, so now she works hard as a volunteer so she can have an impact on someone else.

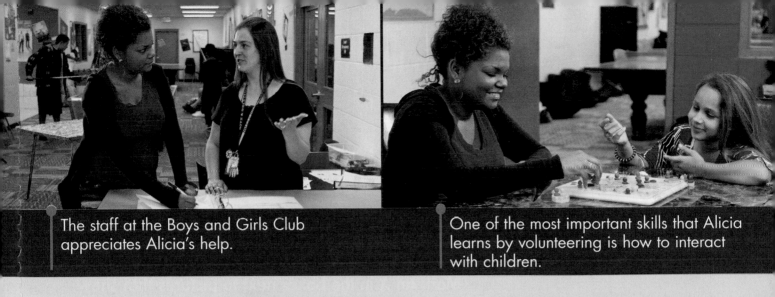

The staff at the Boys and Girls Club appreciates Alicia's help.

One of the most important skills that Alicia learns by volunteering is how to interact with children.

Volunteering is part of being a good citizen. As a volunteer, Alicia contributes to the club's success. "The teens that volunteer here get experience," she explains, "and in return the staff gets help with the hard work." The club staff, or the group of people that works there, is very small. They appreciate the volunteers' help, and so do the children.

While volunteering has given Alicia the chance to help others in the community, it also gives her a chance to grow in different ways. "Some of the skills I learn here, especially interacting with the kids, you can't find in a book."

As she gets ready for college, she realizes that her volunteer work is something great to include in her college admission applications. Alicia is even thinking further into her future. "Almost everyone in my family has served in the military," she tells us. "Someday, I'd like to serve my country too, but not until after college." Volunteering can teach us skills we can use for the rest of our lives.

Think About It Based on this story, do you think you would like to volunteer when you are older? As you read the chapter ahead, think about what Alicia's story tells you about being a good citizen.

Alicia and Kareena had a great time playing basketball.

Good Citizens, Good Deeds

Envision It!

Mark an *X* in the boxes next to pictures that show children being helpful.

As a member of a community, a state, or a nation, you are a citizen. Good citizens behave in ways that help their communities. They set good examples for others. How do you know when you are being a good citizen? Let's find out.

Being a Good Citizen

You welcome the new family that moves in next door. You help carry a neighbor's groceries. A storm leaves branches all over the sidewalk. You pick them up. These are all actions of a good citizen. You are doing good deeds. A **deed** is an action. A good deed is an action that helps others.

Many citizens in communities do good deeds. When the fire department in a community needs a new fire truck, citizens sometimes raise money to buy one. When a community decides to plant a garden with vegetables for citizens to share, people join together to plant the seeds. When people are needed to read to children at the library, some citizens offer to spend their free time doing so. Often, citizens work together for the good of all the people who live in a community.

Good citizens help people in their community.

160

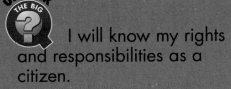
Vocabulary

deed
amendment
volunteer

People in the community notice how other citizens behave and what they do. Good citizens are role models in the community. This means they set good examples for others to follow.

1. **Draw** how you can be a good citizen.

This good citizen is using his free time to read to children at the library.

Our Rights

Citizens of the United States have many rights. Some of these rights were part of the United States Constitution when it was first written. The Constitution is our country's plan of government.

Some people thought that the Constitution needed to include more basic rights of citizens. As a result, ten **amendments,** or changes, were added to the Constitution in 1791. These ten amendments are called the Bill of Rights. The Bill of Rights protects some basic rights of citizens.

The Bill of Rights gives people the right to practice the religion of their choice or no religion. It gives them the right to speak and write their opinions. Citizens also have the right to a fair, legal trial if charged with a crime. The Bill of Rights also gives people the freedom to gather in peaceful groups in public to speak about issues that concern them.

In the United States, one of the most important rights citizens have is the right to vote. Citizens vote to elect leaders. These leaders run our government. Citizens also vote on important issues, such as how the government should spend its money.

Bill of Rights

2. **Look** at the picture. **Write** what the girl might be voting for at her school.

   ....

   ....

   ....

   ....

Good citizens vote on important issues, even at school!

162

Our Responsibilities

Voting is both a right and a responsibility of good citizens. A responsibility is a duty, or something that must be done. The study of the rights and duties of citizens is called civics. By voting in school elections, students help make decisions. When citizens are 18 years old, they can vote for community leaders, such as the mayor. They can also vote for state and national leaders, such as the governor or the president.

Good citizens have other responsibilities, too. For example, they should respect the rights and property of others. If you wait patiently at the water fountain, you are respecting the rights of others. If you give back a classmate's pencil that you borrowed, you are respecting the property of others.

Good citizens have a responsibility to their community. Some citizens are volunteers. A **volunteer** improves the community and helps others. Volunteers work for no pay. They can work in soup kitchens, they can collect clothing for the homeless, or they can bring meals to people who are too sick to leave their homes. Volunteers can help clean up parks and sidewalks. They help because it is something they want to do.

Some people volunteer to help people who need food.

3. List three ways to show good citizenship.

....

....

Our Rules and Laws

We have rules at home and at school. Some families have a rule that everyone must make his or her own bed. That kind of rule helps keep things neat and clean. Schools often have a rule that says students must walk, not run, in the hallways. If students do not follow this rule, they could get hurt.

People follow community laws so that everyone stays safe.

We have laws in our communities. Governments make laws for the common good of all people. Some of those laws help keep us safe. For example, a community may have a law that says people must cross the street at a crosswalk. This community law makes crossing the street safe.

Rules and laws help us to know what to do. They help keep order. Suppose students in a classroom shouted out answers whenever they wanted. It would be difficult to get anything done. That is why there is a rule to raise your hand if you want to speak.

Some people choose not to follow rules or obey laws. They put their safety and the safety of others at risk. At times, people who disobey laws may have to pay a fine or even go to jail.

It is important for all citizens to follow rules and laws. Rules and laws help make our community, state, and nation a safe and orderly place to live.

Students raise their hands so everyone can take turns speaking in class.

4. **Summarize** **Describe** two rules or laws and **explain** how each helps people in a community.

....

....

....

....

....

Got it?

5. **Fact and Opinion** **Read** each statement. **Decide** if it is a fact or an opinion. Then **write** "fact" or "opinion" next to each statement.

.... School hallways are safer when everyone walks.

.... I think there should be a rule that everyone in our class has to clean their desks before they go home.

.... Making your bed helps keep your room neat.

6. **Think** about a good deed you have done. **Write** about what you learned from doing that good deed.

my Story Ideas

....

....

....

Stop! I need help with ....

Wait! I have a question about ....

Go! Now I know ....

Collaboration and Creativity

Conflict and Cooperation

Sometimes when people do not agree, there is a conflict. A conflict is a strong disagreement. For example, there might be a conflict when classmates disagree about who uses the computer first. When there is a conflict, it is important to find a resolution that helps everyone get along. A resolution is a way to resolve a conflict. You can resolve a conflict by cooperating, or working together.

Read the steps below. Then read the paragraph to see how one conflict was resolved.

Steps to Resolving a Conflict

Step 1 Identify the conflict.

Step 2 Calmly tell how you feel, and listen to the other person.

Step 3 Cooperate to find a resolution. If you need to, ask an adult for help to find a resolution.

Harry and Ann finished their animal drawings. Harry wanted to use cotton balls to make wool for his sheep. Ann wanted to use the same cotton balls to make tails for her rabbits. They realized that there was a conflict. How could they resolve this conflict? They calmly talked to each other to find a resolution. Ann used three cotton balls for the rabbits' tails. Harry took the rest and spread them apart to make sheep wool. Harry and Ann cooperated to find a good way to solve their conflict.

Resolving Conflicts

Step 1

Step 2

Step 3

Learning Objective

I will know how to use cooperation to find a resolution to a conflict.

Read the paragraph. Then **answer** the questions.

Aiden and Maria both need to use the classroom computer. They get to the classroom computer at the same time. When Aiden pulls out the chair to sit at the computer, Maria rushes to sit down in the chair. Aiden and Maria are having a conflict.

1. **Write** the conflict Aiden and Maria are having.

....

....

....

2. **Write** what Aiden and Maria should do to resolve the conflict.

....

....

....

....

3. **Write** a resolution to Aiden and Maria's conflict.

....

....

....

Taking Action for Our Rights

People have the right to say what they think and feel as long as it is not harmful to others.

Today, citizens have many rights and freedoms. But these rights and freedoms did not come easily. Throughout history, both famous leaders and ordinary people have worked hard to make sure everyone is treated equally.

Susan B. Anthony

Even after the Bill of Rights was added to the U.S. Constitution, women did not have the same rights as men. Susan B. Anthony wanted to change that. As a young adult, she went to meetings and gave speeches about treating people fairly.

In 1848, Elizabeth Cady Stanton, Lucretia Mott, and other women organized a **convention**, or a large meeting. They wanted to discuss women's rights. A large group of people met in Seneca Falls, New York. One right the women wanted was **suffrage**, or the right to vote. It was the first time that women gathered in public to demand the right to vote. The Seneca Falls Convention was the start of the suffrage movement.

Three years later, in 1851, Susan B. Anthony joined her friend Elizabeth Cady Stanton in the suffrage movement.

In 1880, Susan B. Anthony spoke at a suffrage meeting in Chicago, Illinois.

_____

_____

_____

_____

_____

Write what you think the student in the picture might be speaking about.

UNLOCK
THE BIG
?
I will know about people who fought for the rights and freedoms of our country's citizens.

Vocabulary
....
convention   segregate
suffrage   delegate
civil rights

Susan B. Anthony and Elizabeth Cady Stanton worked to form the National American Woman Suffrage Association in 1869. Susan B. Anthony served as the president of this group for eight years.

In 1870, the Fifteenth Amendment to the United States Constitution was passed. It gave African American men the right to vote. Still, women could not vote. In 1872, Anthony voted in the election for U.S. president. This action was against the law, and she was arrested. She also had to pay $100 for breaking the law, but she refused to pay. She felt it was unfair.

After Anthony died in 1906, other women continued the fight. Finally, in 1920, the Nineteenth Amendment became law. Women had won the right to vote!

1. **◉ Fact and Opinion Write** one fact about Susan B. Anthony.

Women voted for the first time in 1920.

....

....

....

Thurgood Marshall

Thurgood Marshall worked hard for civil rights. **Civil rights** are rights of all citizens to be treated equally under the law. Marshall believed that all citizens, not just some citizens, should have civil rights.

Thurgood Marshall

Marshall grew up in Baltimore, Maryland. He often debated at home with his father and brother. People who have different viewpoints often debate, or argue to convince others to agree with them. Marshall continued to debate in college and later became a lawyer. He began to argue in court to change unfair laws.

At this time, laws **segregated**, or separated, African American and white people in many places. These places included theaters, restaurants, and other public places. African American children and white children were segregated in colleges and schools, too. Marshall wanted to end segregation, especially in schools.

Reverend Oliver Brown, an African American, wanted his daughter, Linda, to attend a school for white students. The African American school was far from the Browns' home. Linda Brown had to cross a dangerous railroad track to get there. The white school was close to the Browns' home, but school leaders would not allow Linda to attend. Other African American families joined in the fight for civil rights.

Linda Brown's case was brought before the Supreme Court. Marshall argued this case, trying to convince the Supreme Court justices that school segregation was wrong. His debating skills helped him win the case. In 1954, all nine Supreme Court justices voted to end school segregation. This court case is known as *Brown* versus *Board of Education*.

Marshall continued to protect people's rights. In 1967, President Lyndon B. Johnson chose Marshall to become the first African American Supreme Court justice. He served on the Supreme Court for 24 years.

2. Draw a banner that supports equal rights.

3. A mother and daughter sit on the steps of the Supreme Court after segregation is made illegal. **Circle** the part of the photograph that shows a change in civil rights.

Nettie Hunt explains Brown *versus* Board of Education *to her daughter, Nickie.*

Eleanor Roosevelt

Eleanor Roosevelt worked hard to improve people's lives. Roosevelt was the First Lady, or the wife of the president. Her husband, Franklin D. Roosevelt, was president from 1933 to 1945. While she was the First Lady, Roosevelt traveled all over the world to visit schoolchildren, sick people in hospitals, coal miners, and even people in jail. She told her husband everything she learned about these people. She was aware that all people need basic human rights.

In 1945, Eleanor Roosevelt had the opportunity to work as a leader for human rights. She was chosen to be the American delegate to the United Nations (U.N.). A **delegate** is a person chosen to act for others. The U.N. is a world group that works for peace. While at the U.N., Roosevelt led a group that worked for human rights. The group wrote a bill of rights for all people. It recognized that all people in the world had human rights. They had the right to be treated equally under the law. They had the right to own property and the right to leave their country and then return.

Eleanor Roosevelt visited many children.

4. List some of the human rights that Eleanor Roosevelt worked for.

....

....

....

Got it?

5. ⊙ **Fact and Opinion Read** each statement. **Decide** if it is a fact or an opinion. Then **write** "fact" or "opinion" next to each statement.

.... Eleanor Roosevelt worked for human rights.

.... Thurgood Marshall was the best Supreme Court justice.

.... Susan B. Anthony was the most important woman in American history.

6. ❓ **Choose** one of the leaders you read about in this lesson. **Explain** why he or she is a good citizen.

my Story Ideas

....

....

....

....

⬛ **Stop!** I need help with ....

⏸ **Wait!** I have a question about ....

▶ **Go!** Now I know ....

Fact and Opinion

A fact is something that can be proved true or false. The sentence, "George Washington was the first president of the United States," is a fact. You can prove it by doing research. The sentence, "George Washington was a funny man," is an opinion. An opinion tells someone's feelings, beliefs, or ideas. An opinion cannot be proved true or false.

Read Caroline's letter to her grandmother. Then look at the facts and opinions from the letter in the chart below.

Hi Grandma,

I just got your letter. Do you want to know what I learned in school today? Today we read about leaders. Thurgood Marshall was the greatest leader of all. He was a lawyer. He always argued for good reasons. Marshall worked to end school segregation. He also became the first African American Supreme Court justice. You should read about Thurgood Marshall, too!

Love,
Caroline

Thurgood Marshall

Facts	Opinions
• Marshall was a lawyer. • He worked to end school segregation. • He became the first African American Supreme Court justice.	• Marshall was the greatest leader of all. • He always argued for good reasons. • You should read about Thurgood Marshall, too!

Read the letter Caroline's grandmother wrote. Then **fill in** the chart with two facts and two opinions from the letter.

Hi Caroline,

I agree with you. I think that Thurgood Marshall was special. I read about leaders in the library today. I read about Eleanor Roosevelt. She was another great leader. She was the First Lady from 1933 to 1945. Her husband, Franklin Delano Roosevelt, was president at that time. Mrs. Roosevelt wanted equal rights for all people. I think we'll have a lot of fun learning about leaders when you visit.

With love,
Grandma

Eleanor Roosevelt

Facts	Opinions

Taking Action for a Cause

Envision It!

ADOPT A PET

Look at the picture. Explain what the girl is doing at the animal shelter.

Many people in our country and all over the world give their support to different causes. A **cause** is something that people feel strongly about. Some people work for world peace, others work to protect Earth, and some groups raise money for research to help cure diseases. People and organizations join together to work for good causes.

Mary McLeod Bethune with a group of students

Mary McLeod Bethune

Mary McLeod Bethune wanted to give African American girls a chance to go to school. She wanted to open a school in Daytona Beach, Florida. The only money she had was $1.50, yet Bethune would not give up on this important cause.

In 1904, Bethune opened her school. It was called the Daytona Normal and Industrial Institute. At her school, Bethune taught African American girls how to read and write. She used old boxes for desks, burned twigs for pencils, and mashed berries for ink. The girls also learned to cook, sew, and clean. Bethune wanted her students to be good citizens, so they worked in the community, too.

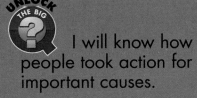
Vocabulary

cause   strike

union   boycott

motto

People from the community donated money to Bethune's cause. In 1923, Bethune's school was able to join with a school for boys called the Cookman Institute. The new school later became Bethune-Cookman College.

Next, Mary McLeod Bethune created an organization for African American women. The organization worked to get African American women better housing, better working conditions, and, of course, a better education. Bethune worked hard to make this organization successful.

In 1936, President Franklin D. Roosevelt asked Bethune to lead the National Youth Administration (NYA). It was a great honor for Bethune. The NYA helped young people find part-time jobs, and Bethune helped by providing job training.

Today, students still attend Bethune's school, now called Bethune-Cookman University. Mary McLeod Bethune is a role model for the students and everyone who has a good cause to support.

1. **⊙ Fact and Opinion Underline** three facts about Mary McLeod Bethune.

A National Youth Administration student

César Chávez

César Chávez knew about the hard lives of farmworkers. When he was a child, Chávez and his family traveled from one farm to another to pick crops. They were paid very little. They had to work long hours. Chávez later served in the United States military. After serving for two years, he went back to work in the fields with other Mexican Americans. But life was not better, so he took up the cause to help farmworkers have better lives.

César Chávez meets with farmworkers.

Many kinds of workers have unions. A **union** is a group of workers that joins together. The workers usually want better treatment and better pay. Chávez felt farmworkers needed a union.

In 1962, Chávez started the National Farm Workers Association (NFWA). It was the first union for farmworkers in America. Chávez was elected president of the NFWA. Later, the name was changed to United Farm Workers. The union's **motto,** or saying, was *Viva la Causa.* This means "Long Live the Cause." Chávez convinced many people to join the farmworkers' cause. He told them that he believed in making changes in peaceful ways. Chávez gave speeches and led marches.

Farm owners were not treating workers who picked grapes fairly. They cut the workers' pay. Chávez wanted to bring attention to these farmworkers' problems.

In 1965, he led the union's first strike. A **strike** happens when workers stop working until things change. These farmworkers refused to pick grapes. The farm owners were angry because they lost money.

Chávez started a boycott. A **boycott** happens when people refuse to do something for a reason. Chávez asked customers to stop buying grapes. He wanted stores to stop selling grapes, too. Many people, and even other workers' unions, helped with the strike.

The farmworkers' strike went on for several years. In 1968, Chávez stopped eating for 25 days! Chávez did this because he wanted people to remember the farmworkers' problems. He also wanted to show workers how to work for a cause in a peaceful way.

Finally, the farm owners agreed to raise the workers' pay. The workers went back to picking grapes. The conflict was resolved peacefully.

People wore pins like this one to support the grape boycott.

2. Explain why Chávez wanted people to boycott grapes.

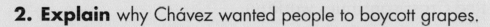

César Chávez leads a group of workers on strike in California.

Clara Barton

In the mid-1800s, Clara Barton volunteered during the American Civil War by helping soldiers find lost baggage and by handing out medicine. The American Civil War was fought between the northern and southern states in our country. Barton also cared for wounded soldiers. She was often called "the angel of the battlefield."

Later, while Barton was in Europe, a war broke out between France and Germany. Barton worked for the Red Cross in Europe, taking care of soldiers who were hurt. She wanted to start the Red Cross in the United States. Barton's wish came true in 1881.

Clara Barton

Today, the American Red Cross continues working for Barton's cause by helping and caring for people all over the world. Red Cross workers arrive quickly to help people after dangerous storms, floods, or earthquakes. They provide food, shelter, clean water, and medicine. The Red Cross makes sure that there is a supply of blood ready for people who need it. The Red Cross also helps people stay in touch with family members in the United States military who are serving our country far from their homes.

American Red Cross workers pack supplies.

3. ◉ **Main Idea and Details Write** one detail that supports the following main idea: Clara Barton helped people.

....

....

....

Got it?

4. ◉ **Fact and Opinion Read** each statement about César Chávez. **Decide** if it is a fact or an opinion. Then **write** "fact" or "opinion" next to each statement.

.... César Chávez started the first union for farmworkers.

.... César Chávez worked for the most important cause.

5. ❓ **Think** about the different examples in this lesson of good citizens working together. **Write** about ways people can make changes when they work together.

(my) **Story Ideas**

....

....

....

....

....

⬛ **Stop!** I need help with ....

⏸ **Wait!** I have a question about ....

▶ **Go!** Now I know ....

Chapter 5

Review and Assessment

Lesson 1

Good Citizens, Good Deeds

1. **Write** three good deeds a citizen might do in the community.

....

....

....

....

2. **Fill in** the chart below. **List** two rights and two responsibilities of citizens.

Rights	Responsibilities

Lesson 2

Taking Action for Our Rights

3. Draw a line to match each leader with the rights that he or she fought for.

Thurgood Marshall   women's right to vote

Eleanor Roosevelt   equal rights for all people

Susan B. Anthony   ending school segregation

4. ⊙ **Fact and Opinion Read** the following statements about Susan B. Anthony. **Label** each statement as a fact or opinion.

.... Susan B. Anthony is someone people should admire.

.... Susan B. Anthony worked with Elizabeth Cady Stanton.

5. Explain what Susan B. Anthony, Thurgood Marshall, and Eleanor Roosevelt had in common.

....

....

....

....

....

....

Lesson 3

Taking Action for a Cause

6. Write a sentence that describes the cause that Mary McLeod Bethune supported.

....

....

....

....

7. Fill in the circle next to the correct answer.

Which of the following means that César Chávez wanted people to stop buying grapes?

○ He joined the military.

○ He picked crops as a child.

○ He started a boycott.

○ He formed a union.

8. Explain how the American Red Cross helps people after dangerous storms and floods.

....

....

....

....

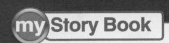

Go online to write and illustrate your own **myStory Book** using the **myStory Ideas** from this chapter.

How can I participate?

In this chapter, you have learned about citizenship. You learned about ways you can participate in your school, in your community, and in your country.

Think about how you can help others in your community.
Write about one way you can make a difference today.

....

....

....

....

Now **draw** a picture of something you can do when you get older to make a difference in your school or in your community.

While you're online, check out the **myStory Current Events** area where you can create your own book on a topic that's in the news.

A Growing Nation

my Story Spark

How does life change throughout history?

Look at the picture on the computer screen of a classroom from about 60 years ago. **Describe** how your classroom looks like this classroom and how it looks different.

....

....

....

....

Benjamin Franklin
A Man Who Changed History

my Story Video

Benjamin Franklin started working for his brother in 1718 when he was 12 years old. His brother owned a print shop in Boston, Massachusetts. The shop printed a newspaper. The job was difficult, but Franklin enjoyed it.

Franklin started writing pieces that were printed in the newspaper. People enjoyed his writing. That is how he learned that being a good writer is a powerful skill.

Later, Franklin moved to Philadelphia, Pennsylvania, and opened his own print shop. Then he wrote a book called an almanac. His almanac gave colonists information, advice, and weather reports.

Franklin thought that working to help people was the best work to do. He worked on many projects that helped the people living in the American colonies.

Benjamin Franklin's work in a print shop showed him that writing is an important skill.

Benjamin Franklin and his friends started a library so they could share books with others.

Franklin's fire company fought fires in people's homes and barns.

One way Franklin helped people was by opening a public library. In the 1730s, only wealthy people owned books. However, Franklin and a few other people asked 50 friends to give them a small amount of money. They used this money to buy books. Then they started a library where people could borrow books to read at home. Today, almost every town in the United States has a public library.

Franklin worked on other projects, too. He started a company to fight fires. He also started an insurance company. The insurance company helped people fix homes that were harmed by fire. Later, Franklin started a hospital. All of these projects helped change Philadelphia.

Science was another subject he enjoyed. In the early 1750s, Franklin found that lightning is a form of electricity. He then created the lightning rod to help keep buildings safe during storms.

In the early 1780s, Franklin had trouble both reading and seeing far away. To solve his problem, he made eyeglasses called bifocals. Bifocals allow people to see both near and far.

Franklin's lightning rods give lightning a path to the ground, keeping buildings safe.

Franklin traveled to France. Many people were excited to meet him.

Franklin helped to write the Declaration of Independence in 1776.

Franklin's work helping people and the new items he created made him famous. Many people wanted to meet him. They painted pictures of him. They asked for his advice.

He traveled to Great Britain and France. When he was in Great Britain, Franklin tried to explain that the American colonists were very angry with the British. He wrote letters about the problems in the American colonies. But the British would not agree to change the laws that the colonists thought were unfair.

Finally, Franklin joined with other American colonial leaders. They all agreed that the colonies should be free from Great Britain. They also agreed that they needed to choose their own leaders. Franklin helped to write the Declaration of Independence. Later, he helped to write the United States Constitution.

During the 1800s, Franklin's work changed life in America in many ways. Even today, we can still see his ideas at work around us.

Think About It Based on this story, how did Benjamin Franklin change life in America? As you read the chapter ahead, think about how helping others has changed people's lives throughout history.

New Ways to Travel

Mark an *X* under the kinds of transportation you have used to get from one place to another.

How do you travel from one place to another? You probably walk or ride in a car or bus. Long ago, explorers and settlers traveled by boat and by foot as they tried to learn about new lands.

Travel by Trails and Rivers

When Europeans arrived in North America in the 1500s, they knew nothing about the land. However, Native Americans knew the land well. They traveled by boat on rivers and by foot on trails they had made. They showed Europeans where to find what they needed. Later, explorers from Spain brought horses to North America. Horses made travel easier and faster.

As the country grew, many people wanted to explore the West. In 1803, President Thomas Jefferson hired Meriwether Lewis and William Clark to explore the land west of the Mississippi River. He asked them to learn about the Native Americans and the land in the West.

Lewis and Clark traveled with about 48 other men. Sacagawea (sak uh juh WEE uh) was a Native American who helped them understand the language of the Native Americans they met.

Boats helped Lewis and Clark explore the West.

I will know how new ways of traveling have changed people's lives.

Vocabulary

canal
wagon train
transcontinental
toll

It took two years for Lewis and Clark to finish their trip. The map below shows where they went.

Their stories made many people want to move west. People heard about the huge open spaces and the chance of getting land they could farm. Because of Lewis and Clark, many people traveled to the West and set up new communities.

1. **Use** the map scale to **measure** about how many miles Lewis and Clark traveled on their route.

....

....

....

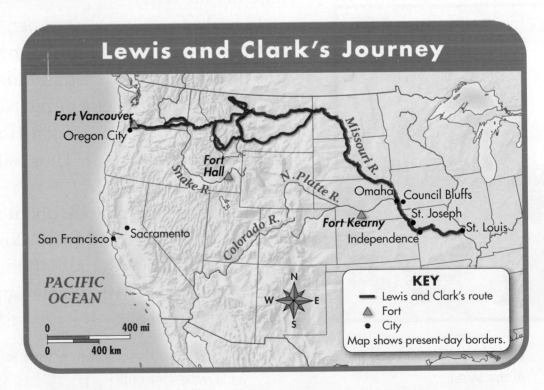

Lewis and Clark's Journey

Fort Vancouver
Oregon City
Snake R.
Fort Hall
N. Platte R.
Missouri R.
Omaha Council Bluffs
St. Joseph
Colorado R.
Fort Kearny
St. Louis
San Francisco Sacramento
Independence

PACIFIC OCEAN

0   400 mi
0   400 km

KEY
—— Lewis and Clark's route
▲ Fort
● City
Map shows present-day borders.

Rivers and Canals

In the early 1800s, rivers were an important way to carry heavy goods. However, some rivers were too narrow or too fast for big boats. Sometimes a canal was built to let boats get through safely. A **canal** is a waterway that is dug by people.

In 1825, the Erie Canal helped connect the Great Lakes to New York City. Goods from what are now Wisconsin and Michigan were shipped over the Great Lakes. The goods were then carried down the Erie Canal to the Hudson River and then on to New York City. Soon, New York City became an important port. A port is a town or city that has a place for ships to land.

The Erie Canal improved transportation of goods and people.

Wagon Trains

Another form of transportation in the early 1800s was the covered wagon. Many people traveled to the West in wagon trains. A **wagon train** is a group of covered wagons that travels together for safety.

To make traveling west easier, Congress built the National Road. Many families began their trip on this paved road. It started in Maryland and ended in Illinois. From the end of the National Road, people traveled to the Oregon Trail, which began in Independence, Missouri. They followed this trail to Oregon.

The trip to Oregon took about six months. People faced harsh weather, sickness, and steep mountains. Although more than 12,000 people went west in the 1840s, a safer and faster way to travel was needed.

People walked or rode in wagons to find a better life in the West.

2. **Underline** the sentence that tells about how the trip west was difficult.

The Oregon Trail and National Road

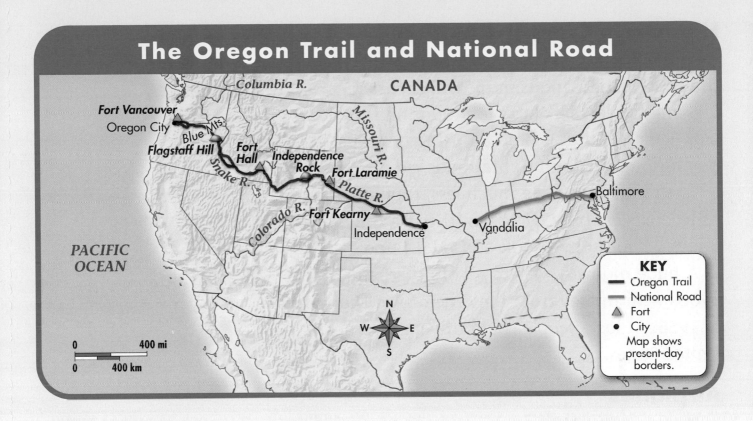

Railroads Cross the Country

The first steam locomotive was built in 1804. Steam locomotives are trains that run with steam engines. As improvements were made over the next ten years, they became powerful and could go long distances. Soon, people began planning railroads.

In 1863, two companies began building a railroad line across America. One company began in the East and one in the West. On May 10, 1869, the two lines met in Promontory, Utah. The new railroad was called the transcontinental railroad. **Transcontinental** means "across the continent."

Railroads were a big improvement over slow canal boats, muddy roads, and narrow trails. Now, people could travel quickly and safely from Omaha, Nebraska, to Sacramento, California.

A gold spike joined the eastern and western rail lines.

3. **Underline** the sentence that tells where the transcontinental railroad started and ended.

Highways Cross the Nation

Many new roads were built in the United States in the 1800s. These roads made travel easier.

Some landowners built toll roads on their land. A **toll** is money that is paid for using a road. Tolls helped pay for building and fixing roads.

The roads were used much less, though, after railroads were built. However, they became important again when many people started driving cars.

A huge highway system was finally built in the 1900s with money from the Federal-Aid Highway Act of 1956. At last, people could travel easily across the United States.

Airplanes

In the early 1900s, transportation continued to improve. Two brothers, Orville and Wilbur Wright, began building airplanes. On December 17, 1903, their first airplane flew. It stayed in the air for 12 seconds. Suddenly, people could fly!

The Wright brothers kept improving their design. The idea of traveling by airplane became popular.

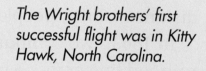

The Wright brothers' first successful flight was in Kitty Hawk, North Carolina.

Over the years, airplanes grew larger and more powerful. Today, jets carry people and items all over the world. A trip across the country, which once took months, now takes less than six hours.

4. ⊙ **Draw Conclusions Explain** how travel changed in the 1900s.

....

....

5. ⊙ **Draw Conclusions Read** each statement. Then **write** a conclusion you can draw about each statement.

Wagon trains helped people travel safely.

....

....

Railroads were a big improvement over muddy roads.

....

....

Highways helped people travel across the United States.

....

....

6. ❓ **Explain** why wagon trains were the best way to travel across the country in the 1800s.

my Story Ideas

....

....

....

⬛ **Stop!** I need help with ....

⏸ **Wait!** I have a question about ....

▶ **Go!** Now I know ....

Primary and Secondary Sources

Primary sources are documents, such as photographs, paintings, and maps, or artifacts from the time an event happened. Primary sources were written or used by someone who saw or lived through an event. Sometimes that person is called an "eyewitness."

The primary sources on this page are from Lewis and Clark's journey. They used the compass to help them find their way. The journal entry was written by John Ordway, who traveled with Lewis and Clark.

Read the journal entry below. As you read, think about who created it and why. Also think about what it tells you about the past.

Artifacts like compasses can be primary sources.

> one of the hunters...killed a panther on an island. It was 7 1/2 feet in length. it differs from these in the States. it is of a redish brown. and the first we have killed. passed very rapid water we have to double man the canoes and drag them over the Sholes and rapid places. we have to be in the water half of our time.
>
> August 3. 1805. John Ordway

Journals are primary sources, too.

What does Ordway's journal tell you about Lewis and Clark's journey? What did he see? How are the words and spellings in the journal different from the way people write today?

Learning Objective

I will know the differences between primary and secondary sources.

This passage from a textbook also tells about Lewis and Clark's journey. But it was written by someone who learned about the trip by reading other people's writings. It is a secondary source. In secondary sources, the author did not see or live through the events he or she describes.

This book is a secondary source.

The members of the Lewis and Clark expedition faced many dangers. The explorers followed rivers that were often very narrow or rapid.

They brought back examples of the plants and animals they found to show people what they found in the West.

Try it!

1. **Describe** how the journal entry is different from the textbook passage.

   ....

   ....

   ....

   ....

2. **Use** the Internet to find more information about Lewis and Clark's journey. **Describe** the information you find and **tell** if it is from a primary source or a secondary source.

   ....

   ....

A New Home in America

Envision It!

List the items you would pack in your bag if you were moving to a new home.

Many jobs were available in the United States.

People move to a new place for many reasons. Some need to find work. Some want freedom or a safe place to live. Some hope to earn more money. Some move to be closer to their family.

The Promise of America

People who move from one country to settle in a different country are called **immigrants.** Immigrants started coming to North America hundreds of years ago to start new lives.

Some of the first immigrants were people from Spain, France, and England. In the 1600s and 1700s, they crossed the Atlantic Ocean to come to North America. They settled in the Southeast, the Northeast, and even as far north as Canada.

In 1783, the United States won its freedom from Great Britain. At that time, the nation was made up of 13 states, and all of the states were located in the East.

The West was a huge open land with many rivers and mountains. The soil was rich for farming, and gold could be found in the streams and rocks. While people were looking for gold, they also found other minerals, such as silver. People found many ways to earn money in the West.

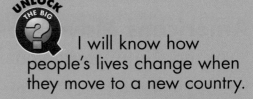
Vocabulary
· ·

immigrant   gold rush
frontier   exclusion
homestead

In the mid-1800s, thousands of immigrants from Europe and Asia came to the United States. Most settled in cities along the East and West coasts where there were many jobs and places to live. Other immigrants bought or rented land to farm.

Since the first Europeans arrived in North America, immigrants have had high hopes for their new home. They brought the skills and energy needed to make the country even greater.

One immigrant, John Roebling (ROH blihng), came from Germany to the United States in 1831. He built many bridges. One of his best-known bridges is the Brooklyn Bridge in New York City.

Most European immigrants sailed across the Atlantic Ocean and into New York Harbor. One of the first things they saw there was the Statue of Liberty. Even today, it welcomes immigrants.

1. ◎ **Cause and Effect Write** two causes of immigrants settling in the West.

....

....

....

The Statue of Liberty holds a lamp to welcome people to the United States.

Americans Move West

As more immigrants came and cities became crowded, many people looked for more land in the American frontier. A **frontier** is a region that forms the edge of a settled area. People crossed steep mountains and wide rivers. The search for more land was dangerous. An explorer named Daniel Boone helped make this search easier.

The Cumberland Gap trail had been used by Native Americans for many years. It ran through the Cumberland Mountains. The map below shows the Cumberland Gap trail today.

In 1775, Boone worked with 28 men to widen the Cumberland Gap trail and add new paths. This new road was called the Wilderness Road. Wagons could now travel through the mountains. As a result, thousands of settlers and explorers traveled west, beyond the Appalachian Mountains. In 1805, Zebulon Pike (ZEB yuh lun pyk) explored the Mississippi River. Davy Crockett began exploring present-day Tennessee in 1813.

Daniel Boone helped new settlers travel to the American frontier.

2. **Look** at the map. **Circle** the three states that meet in the Cumberland Gap trail.

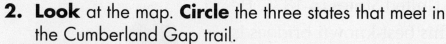

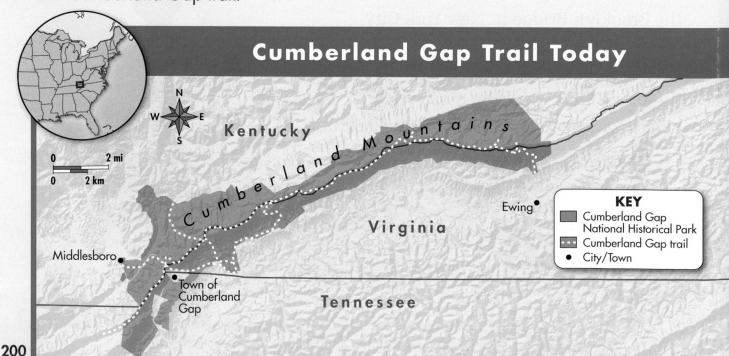

Cumberland Gap Trail Today

Kentucky

Cumberland Mountains

0   2 mi
0   2 km

Ewing

Virginia

Middlesboro

Town of Cumberland Gap

Tennessee

KEY
- Cumberland Gap National Historical Park
- Cumberland Gap trail
- City/Town

The Homestead Act

The number of settlers moving west grew after 1862. In that year, the U.S. government passed the Homestead Act. A **homestead** is an area of land that includes a house and its buildings.

The Homestead Act made it possible for many Americans to get 160 acres of land for very little money. The act helped people settle the land in the West. It also helped the country add new states.

To be a homesteader, a person had to agree to build a house and live on the land for five years. After that, the person would own the land. Thousands of families traveled west to find a new home. By the 1900s, there were 600,000 homesteaders in the West.

Many homesteaders were immigrants. Others had been slaves in the South. By moving west, people could start new lives. They could farm and feed their families. They could start new communities and enjoy their freedom.

Life for the homesteaders in the West was difficult, though. They built homes using any materials they could find. They carried water in buckets. They grew all of their food. Neighbors were far from each other, so it was difficult to get help. Many people returned home because life on the frontier was so harsh.

Families could buy land to start a new life in the West.

3. ◎ **Draw Conclusions Write** one detail that supports the conclusion that life for the homesteaders was difficult.

....

....

....

Immigrants From Asia

In 1848, gold was discovered in California. During the **gold rush**, thousands of people came from around the world to search for gold.

Many immigrants came from China during the gold rush. At first, Americans welcomed them. However, some Americans thought that Chinese immigrants were taking too many jobs. In 1882, the United States government passed the Chinese Exclusion Act. **Exclusion** means "keeping people out of a place." This act stopped immigration from China for ten years.

In the 1880s, Japan started allowing workers to move to the United States. Many Japanese immigrants lived in California and in Hawaii, which was not yet a state. Most worked on farms or fished. Some owned small businesses. However, Japanese immigrants faced some of the same problems as Chinese immigrants.

Chinese immigrants needed special documents to work in the United States.

4. **Look** at the map. **Circle** the name of the ocean Chinese and Japanese immigrants crossed to reach the United States.

Immigration From China and Japan, 1848–1900

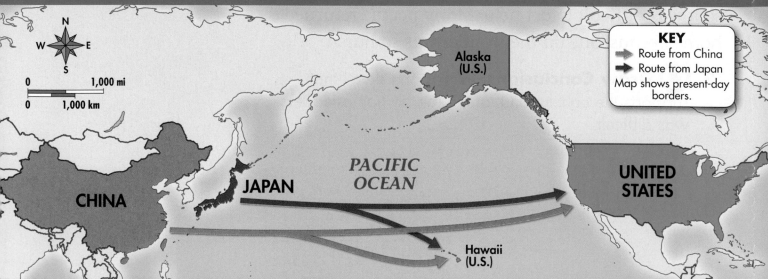

Got it?

5. **Draw Conclusions Use** the facts you learned to draw a conclusion about how each of these examples affected immigrants to the United States.

Wilderness Road: ....

Homestead Act of 1862: ....

Gold Rush: ....

Chinese Exclusion Act of 1882: ....

6. **Describe** what you think it was like to cross the Atlantic Ocean by ship in the 1800s.

my Story Ideas

....

Stop! I need help with ....

Wait! I have a question about ....

Go! Now I know ....

New Ways to Communicate

Envision It!

1800s

Circle the items in each picture that help people communicate.

The Pony Express promised to deliver mail quickly and safely across the United States.

How do we learn about the world around us? We look and listen. We also use tools, such as telephones, radios, televisions, and computers. These tools help people communicate with each other. When people **communicate**, they pass their thoughts or information to others.

The Pony Express

In the early 1800s, the only way to travel across the country was on horseback or by wagon train. Sending letters took anywhere from days to weeks.

As the country grew, the mail service had to improve. In 1860, a group of people set up the Pony Express. The Pony Express was a mail system that carried letters between St. Joseph, Missouri, and Sacramento, California. The map shows the route the mail traveled.

Young men carried mail bags on horseback for 75 to 100 miles. Riders changed horses every ten miles at relay stations.

At the end of their part of the trip, riders waited at their last station for another rider coming from the opposite direction. Then they would pick up that rider's mail bag and ride home.

1950s

UNLOCK THE BIG ?

I will know the different ways people have communicated throughout history.

Vocabulary

communicate   telegraph
invention   technology
patent

Pony Express riders rode through heavy snow and rain. They also kept away from Native Americans who did not want them on their land.

The Pony Express improved how people communicated. Now mail could reach the West Coast in only ten days. The Pony Express lasted only 18 months, as new systems began making communication even faster and easier.

1. Look at the map. **Circle** the places where Pony Express riders may have stopped to change horses.

The Pony Express

KEY
— Pony Express route
🏛 Station
★ Capital city
• City
Map shows present-day borders.

Snake R.
Burnt Ranch
Guinard's Bridge
Missouri R.
Mississippi R.
Platte R.
Rock Creek
Bucklands
Big Mountain Pass
Thirty-two Mile
St. Joseph
San Francisco
Sacramento
Willow Springs
Colorado R.
Hollenberg
Pony Express Stable

PACIFIC OCEAN

0   400 mi
0   400 km

N
W   E
S

Telegraphs and Telephones

New inventions also improved communication. An **invention** is something that is made for the first time. People protect their inventions by getting patents on them. A **patent** gives a person the right to be the only one making or selling an invention.

In 1832, Samuel Morse began work to develop a telegraph. A **telegraph** is a machine that sends and receives signals through a thin wire. Six years later, he invented a special code he called the Morse code. The Morse code uses dots and dashes to represent letters and numbers. Telegraphs used Morse code to deliver messages almost instantly.

In 1844, the first telegraph message was sent between two cities. It was not until 1854, however, that Morse was given a patent for his invention.

Alexander Graham Bell, who was originally from Scotland, liked the telegraph. He wondered, though, if he could send the human voice through wires. In 1876, Bell invented the telephone. For the first time, people could talk without seeing each other.

2. **Underline** the sentence that tells how the telephone affected how people communicated.

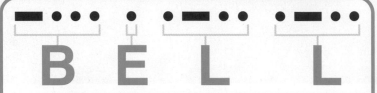

This is how Alexander Graham Bell's name would be sent in Morse code.

Alexander Graham Bell makes the first telephone call from New York City to Chicago, Illinois.

206

Radio and Television

The telegraph and the telephone helped people communicate over long distances. However, these inventions used wires that were strung between buildings or cities. In 1896, Italian inventor Guglielmo Marconi (goo LYEL moh mahr KOH nee) found a way to send messages without wires.

Marconi patented a way for radio signals to travel through the air. People could now send and receive messages without telegraph wires.

In 1901, he received the first radio message sent across the Atlantic Ocean. Suddenly, people around the world could communicate instantly.

Many inventions were created by one person. However, some were developed by many people. The television was one of these inventions. The idea for the television is based on the work of Morse, Bell, Marconi, and many other scientists. Each one created parts of the new machine.

Although the creation of today's televisions took many years, most of the work was done in the 1920s and 1930s. In 1939, the television was introduced to a large audience at the World's Fair in New York. By the late 1940s, many Americans owned a television. These televisions showed black-and-white pictures. Since then, many scientists have improved the television.

Today, almost every home in the United States has at least one television. In addition, people can watch television through their computers and other communication tools.

3. ◉ **Sequence Look** at the pictures of communication tools. **Number** them 1–4 in the order they were invented.

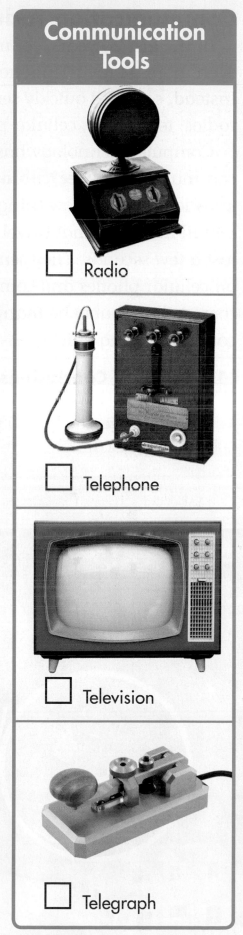

Communication Tools

☐ Radio

☐ Telephone

☐ Television

☐ Telegraph

Communication Today

In the last 20 years, communication has changed even more. Many telephones do not use wires. Instead, satellites quickly send and receive signals for radios, televisions, cellular phones, and computers.

Computer technology has also improved communication. **Technology** is the scientific knowledge about how things work. People write e-mail messages that travel around the world in just a few seconds. They send photos and videos on cellular phones and computers. In the future, there will probably be many more new ways of communicating quickly.

4. ⊙ **Draw Conclusions Write** one detail that supports the conclusion that communication has changed over the last 20 years.

....

....

Satellites send and receive signals to make communication faster.

5. ⊙ **Draw Conclusions Write** a conclusion you can draw about how each type of communication has changed the way people live.

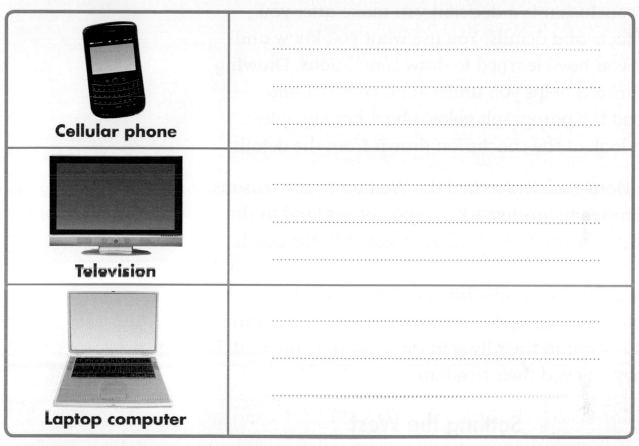

Cellular phone	....
Television	....
Laptop computer	....

6. ❓ **Describe** how people communicated with each other before the invention of the telephone and how the telephone made communication easier.

my Story Ideas

....

....

....

⏹ **Stop!** I need help with ....

⏸ **Wait!** I have a question about ....

▶ **Go!** Now I know ....

Reading Skills

Draw Conclusions

A conclusion is a decision you make after you read facts and details. You use what you know and what you have learned to draw conclusions. Drawing conclusions helps you understand your reading.

Read the paragraph below about homesteaders. Then look at the conclusion drawn from the details.

Homesteaders settled the West for many reasons. Some were farmers who could not get land in the East to farm. Some had been slaves in the South. They wanted to make new lives for themselves and their families. Some homesteaders thought they could get rich by buying cheap land and farming it. Many found their lives in the West were difficult, but they enjoyed their freedom.

Settling the West

Details	Conclusion
1. Farmers had no land in the East. 2. People who had been enslaved wanted to start new lives. 3. People wanted to get rich.	People became homesteaders in the West because they wanted a better life.

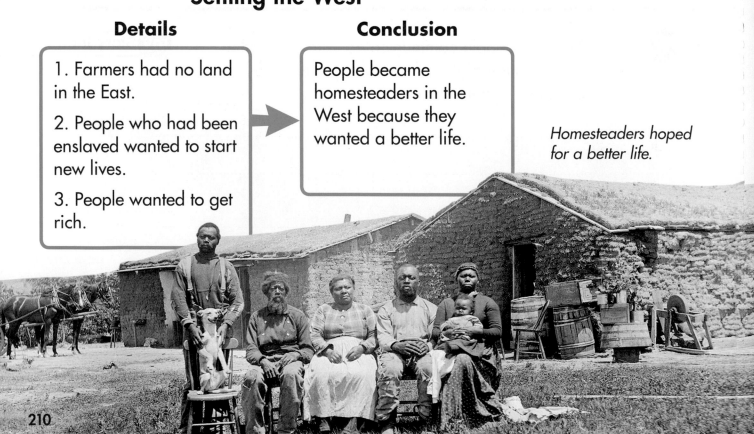

Homesteaders hoped for a better life.

210

Read the passage about the Pony Express. Then **answer** the question.

A Pony Express rider is on his way to deliver mail.

    The Pony Express was created during the Civil War to help people find out what was happening around the country. Before the Pony Express, the mail had been carried by stagecoach and by boat.

    Pony Express riders risked their lives to deliver the mail. They rode as fast as they could, and they did not rest very often.

    Mail delivery was much faster with the Pony Express, but it was not safe enough or fast enough. The Pony Express went out of business after the telegraph was invented.

Fill in the chart with two more details about the Pony Express riders. Then **fill in** the chart with a conclusion you can draw from the details.

The Pony Express Riders

Details	Conclusion
1. Riders risked their lives. 2. .... 3.	....

New Ideas

Light

Washing machine

Circle the inventions that help you to keep clean.

Throughout history, new ideas have changed people's lives. Some kinds of ideas involve making new things, such as cars. Others involve creating new ways to live. Both kinds of ideas can change the way people lead their lives.

In the late 1800s and early 1900s, more people began to work to give all Americans equal rights. When people have **equal rights**, they have the same rights as others.

Women wanted the right to vote. African Americans wanted their children to have the right to go to the same schools as white children. Workers wanted rules to keep them safe. Many Americans worked to turn these ideas into laws.

Education and New Inventions

In the early 1900s, many schools were segregated. White and African American students went to separate schools. Sometimes no schools were available for African American children.

Some people thought this was wrong. They wanted all children to have equal educations. In 1904, Mary McLeod Bethune opened a school for African American girls in Florida.

Mary McLeod Bethune helped African American girls get an education.

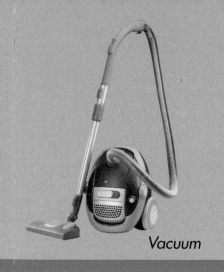
Vacuum

Refrigerator

UNLOCK THE BIG ?

I will know how new ideas and machines changed people's lives throughout history.

Vocabulary

equal rights
assembly line
vaccine
activist

In 1954, the United States Supreme Court ruled that school segregation was against the law. Now all children could have equal educations.

In the 1900s, the lives of Americans changed in other ways, too. One big change was caused by the invention of the first practical, or useful, light bulb. In 1879, Thomas Edison had invented a light bulb that was cheap and reliable. It provided light without needing to light a fire or a candle.

It took years for electrical wires to be put in and power stations to be built. However, by the 1900s, factories and offices could stay open at night. People could walk safely on well-lit streets, too.

Today, inventions are still changing people's lives. Cameras and computers have changed the way people communicate, shop for goods, and gather information about the world.

A camera from 2010

A camera from the early 1900s

1. ◉ **Main Idea and Details Underline** three ways that people's lives changed in the 1900s.

New Machines for Work

In 1831, Cyrus Hall McCormick, whose parents came from Scotland and Ireland, invented a machine that cut grain. It was called a reaper. Before, people cut crops by hand. The reaper made cutting grain faster and easier. Today, machines help farmers plant, plow, and harvest crops. They help farmers use more land and grow more crops.

One of the most important inventions of the late 1800s was the automobile, or car. In 1903, Henry Ford opened a business that built and sold cars. At that time, most people could not afford a car.

Ford wanted to build a car that everyone could afford. He looked for a way to save time and money making cars. He thought about each thing a worker had to know to build a car.

This led him to invent the assembly line. On an **assembly line**, each worker does only one part of a job. Ford's assembly line idea was used in factories around the world.

Assembly lines helped Ford make a car called the Model T. The Model T cost less than other cars. Now, millions of people could afford to buy cars.

2. **Underline** the sentence that shows that many factories decided to use Ford's assembly line ideas.

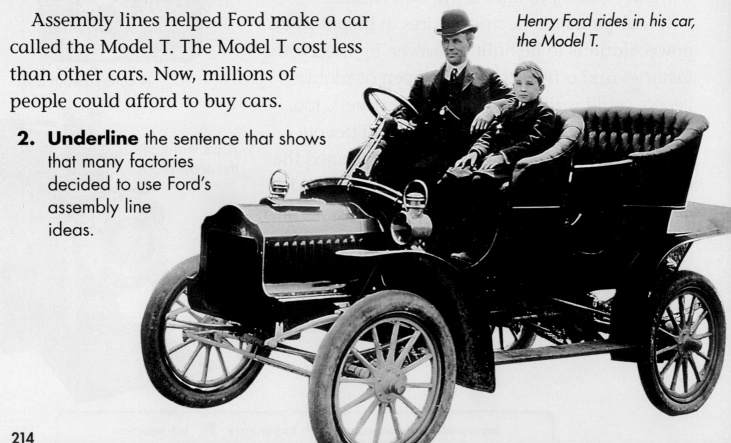

Henry Ford rides in his car, the Model T.

New Ideas in Medicine

In the 1700s, a disease called smallpox killed millions of people. No one knew what caused it. There was no cure.

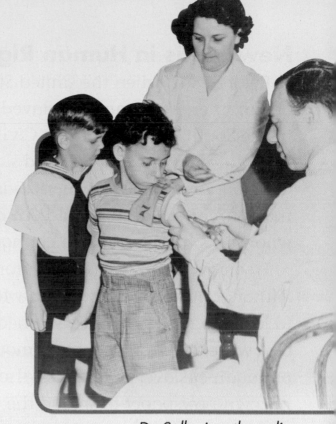

Then in 1796, Edward Jenner found a way to protect people from this terrible disease. He gave them a vaccine made from a very weak virus. A **vaccine** helps people's bodies fight off disease. Jenner's vaccine helped people fight off smallpox.

Polio was another terrible disease. In the 1950s, a Jewish American doctor named Jonas Salk used Jenner's ideas to invent a vaccine against polio. Salk gave people a dead form of the polio virus. Salk's vaccine helped people's bodies learn how to fight off the polio virus. The vaccine saved the lives of many people.

Dr. Salk gives the polio vaccine to a child in 1954.

Louis Pasteur (LOO ee pas TOOR) discovered that many diseases are caused by germs. Pasteur thought that people would not get sick if germs did not enter their bodies. In the 1860s, he invented a way to kill germs by heating foods and cooling them quickly. This process is called pasteurization. Today, most of the milk we drink is pasteurized.

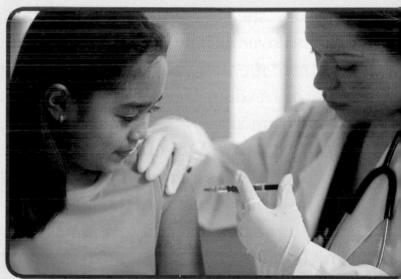

People today get many vaccines to help them stay healthy.

3. ◉ **Main Idea and Details**
Write how a vaccine helps keep people healthy.

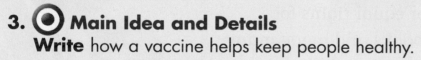

New Ideas in Human Rights

Before 1861, when the United States Civil War began, there were many enslaved African Americans in the South. One reason the Civil War was fought was that many people believed slavery was wrong.

Before and after the war, activists worked to win freedom for enslaved people. An **activist** is someone who works hard to make a change happen.

Frederick Douglass escaped from slavery in 1838. Although it was against the law for enslaved people to learn to read, Douglass learned how to read and write. He soon became famous for speaking out against slavery. Douglass also printed his own newspaper to spread the word that African Americans should be free.

Frederick Douglass

Another activist was Harriet Tubman. She escaped from slavery in 1849. For the next ten years, she kept returning to the South to help enslaved people escape. By 1860, she had freed more than 300 slaves. She risked her own freedom and her life to help others escape from slavery.

Harriet Tubman

After the Civil War ended in 1865, enslaved African Americans were finally free. However, African Americans still did not have the same rights as others. It would take many years and the work of many activists to make this happen.

In the 1950s and 1960s, Martin Luther King Jr. became a leader in the fight for equal rights for African Americans. He wrote books and made many speeches. He led thousands of people in a march on Washington, D.C., where he delivered his famous "I Have a Dream" speech.

Martin Luther King Jr.

Many Americans have worked for equal rights. Some have used their power in government to make changes. In 1964, President Lyndon B. Johnson helped pass a law that made it illegal to treat people differently in the workplace. The lives of many people changed as a result of all of these activists' work.

4. ⊙ **Draw Conclusions Use** the details you have read to **write** a conclusion about equal rights activists.

....

....

Got it?

5. ⊙ **Draw Conclusions Read** the following sentence. Then **write** a conclusion you can draw from it.

For ten years, Harriet Tubman kept returning to the South to help enslaved people escape to freedom.

....

....

6. ❓ **Think** about someone in the early 1900s who is driving a Model T Ford to a friend's house. **Describe** how that trip might be different from a trip you take in a car today.

my Story Ideas

....

....

....

⏹ **Stop!** I need help with ....

⏸ **Wait!** I have a question about ....

▶ **Go!** Now I know ....

Review and Assessment

Lesson 1

New Ways to Travel

1. **Describe** how the National Road led to more people settling the West.

....

....

2. **Explain** how the transcontinental railroad changed the United States.

....

....

3. **Number** the following events 1–4 in the order in which they happened.

_____ The transcontinental railroad is completed.

_____ The Erie Canal is opened.

_____ Lewis and Clark explore the land west of the Mississippi.

_____ The airplane is invented.

Lesson 2

A New Home in America

4. **Write** the different types of jobs that Japanese immigrants did after they arrived in the United States.

....

....

....

Lesson 3

New Ways to Communicate

5. ◉ **Draw Conclusions** **Read** the details. Then **fill in** the chart with a conclusion you can draw from the details.

Details

1. The invention of the telegraph allowed people to send messages almost instantly.

2. The invention of the radio allowed people to send messages to many people at one time without wires.

3. People can now use computers to send e-mail messages instantly.

Conclusion

6. **Write** how each of these inventions changed the way people communicated with one another.

a. Telephone ....

....

b. Television ....

....

Lesson 4

New Ideas

7. **Draw** a line to match each person with his invention.

Jonas Salk	way to kill germs
Henry Ford	reaper
Louis Pasteur	assembly line
Cyrus McCormick	polio vaccine

8. **Fill in** the circle next to the correct answer.

   Who helped pass a law making it illegal to treat people differently in the workplace?

   ○ President Lyndon B. Johnson

   ○ Harriet Tubman

   ○ Frederick Douglass

   ○ Martin Luther King Jr.

9. **Explain** how Edward Jenner helped protect people from smallpox.

   ....

   ....

10. **Write** a detail to support this conclusion: Martin Luther King Jr. worked hard to help African Americans get equal rights.

   ....

   ....

   ....

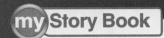

Go online to write and illustrate your own **myStory Book** using the **myStory Ideas** from this chapter.

How does life change throughout history?

Life has changed in many ways over time. Inventions and new ideas in transportation, communication, medicine, and technology have made our lives easier.

Think about how travel and communication have changed over the years. **Write** about the different ways you have traveled or communicated.

....

....

....

....

Now **draw** a picture that shows the way you travel or communicate most often.

While you're online, check out the **myStory Current Events** area where you can create your own book on a topic that's in the news.

Working in Our Communities

How do people get what they need?

Think about the choices people make when they buy things. Then **write** about a choice you made when you bought something.

....

....

....

....

....

Farmers Market
Meet Me at Third and Fairfax

Sloan's eyes light up when he sees Kip's Toyland. "This is the best place on Earth!" he declares. Today, Sloan is visiting Farmers Market at Third and Fairfax in Los Angeles, California. This historic market has been providing goods and services to local customers since 1934. Goods are things that people make or grow and then sell. A service is work that one person does for another.

Sloan was so excited when he arrived at Farmers Market that he did not know what he wanted to see first!

"No toys today, Sloan," says his mom. "We have other things we need to buy." As they head off to explore the market, Sloan notices all of the colorful displays. There is a variety of T-shirts and sweatshirts hanging in one store window, and there is bright, shiny jewelry on display in another window. Looking inside one of the children's stores, Sloan smiles as he finds a play area right in the middle of the store! He stops walking as he takes a moment to enjoy the smell of all the delicious food. "Mmm, I smell Chinese food," he says. "Maybe that's what I'll have for lunch!"

223

There is a wide variety of fruits and vegetables available at Farmers Market.

The butcher shop has many different kinds of meats to choose from.

Sloan could not resist stopping to look at all of the delicious baked goods!

People shop for things they need at the market. Many different people provide goods here at Farmers Market. Local farmers bring their fruits and vegetables so they can sell them directly to the people at the market. This is one of the reasons Sloan and his mom love coming to Farmers Market. Shoppers can be sure that the food they are buying is as fresh as it can be.

Sloan makes his way to the nearest vegetable stand. "There it is . . . broccoli. My favorite!" he tells us. Next to this vegetable stand is a butcher shop. "I really like chicken," Sloan says. There is a shop for just about every type of food you can think of, whether you are looking for meats, cheeses, or even fresh peanut butter. There is also a fish monger, or someone who sells fish and seafood, and several bakeries. If your dog needs a treat, there is even a bakery for him or her!

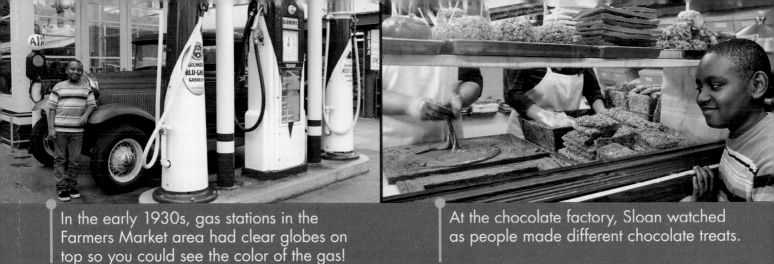

In the early 1930s, gas stations in the Farmers Market area had clear globes on top so you could see the color of the gas!

At the chocolate factory, Sloan watched as people made different chocolate treats.

People can also buy things they want at Farmers Market. There are toy stores, a hat shop, a spice store, and even a chocolate factory. Sloan sees a lot of things he wants, but he decides to ask his mom if she can buy only one of these things for him. "Okay, Sloan, you can have a baseball cap," she tells him. "I'll take that one," Sloan tells the storekeeper. "This is my favorite team. Thank you!"

Farmers Market is right in the middle of a big city. People who live nearby come here to shop, eat, and enjoy street musicians. It is a bustling, busy place. There are plenty of small souvenir stores here, too. A souvenir is something that serves as a reminder. "I had a great time at the market today," Sloan says. "I know I didn't need this souvenir penny, but isn't it neat?" People often buy souvenirs here to remember their trip to Farmers Market. If you could choose a souvenir, what would you choose?

Sloan proudly shows the souvenir penny he made.

Think About It Based on this story, do you think Farmers Market is a good place for people to find what they need and want? As you read the chapter ahead, think about what this story tells you about how people in communities work together to meet their needs and wants.

Meeting Our Needs and Wants

Envision It!

Circle two things that would help you do your work at school.

Clothing and healthful foods are needs.

Have you ever said, "I really need that toy!"? Do you really need it, or do you just want it? There is a difference between needing and wanting.

Needs and Wants

Needs are things you must have to live. Healthful food, water, clothing, and shelter are all needs. You need food and water to live. You need a sweater to stay warm in cold weather. You need a place to live to stay warm, dry, and comfortable.

Wants are things you would like to have but do not need. You can live without them. Basketballs, special sneakers, and board games are wants.

Some things are wants for some people and needs for others. For example, some people want a boat so they can water ski. However, other people need a boat for transportation.

1. Fill in the chart with two needs and two wants.

Needs	Wants

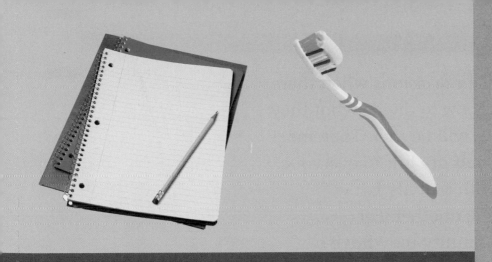

Vocabulary

needs   opportunity
wants   cost
scarcity   value
abundance

Enough or Too Much?

When there is **scarcity**, there is not enough of something to meet people's needs and wants. For example, if it does not rain for a long time, there may be a scarcity of water. Flowers may not bloom and water levels may become low.

When there is scarcity, people must make choices about how to use what they have. If there is not enough water, people might decide not to water their lawns. This will make more water available for washing and drinking.

If there is an **abundance**, there is a lot of something. For example, if it rains for a long time, there might be an abundance of water. When there is an abundance of something, there is enough to meet people's needs and wants.

2. ◎ **Compare and Contrast Explain** the difference between scarcity and abundance.

....

....

....

Little rain might lead to a scarcity of water.

Scarcity and Choice

People have to make difficult decisions when there is scarcity. They must decide how to divide what they have so that everyone's needs will be met. They must find a way to make choices that are fair to everyone.

Some communities deal with scarcity by exchanging products with one another. For example, people in one community may have a lot of vegetables, such as carrots. People in another community may have an abundance of dairy products. These communities might exchange their extra carrots and dairy products so that everyone has what they need.

When there is a scarcity of money, people have to make careful choices about how they will spend what they have. Suppose you have enough money to buy one softball glove or two books about softball. You consider your choices. Your glove is getting old, but it still fits. The books are about your favorite players, and you have been looking forward to reading them. You decide to buy the books.

Sometimes when you make a choice, you have to give something up. You gave up the softball glove when you chose to buy the books. The glove was your opportunity cost. An item's **opportunity cost** is the value of the thing you give up when you choose one thing over another. An item's **value** is what it is worth to a person.

3. ◎ **Main Idea and Details Underline** what people need to do when there is a scarcity of money.

When you exchange something with someone else, you give up one thing to get another thing.

228

Value and Choice

People make choices when they spend money. They decide which item they want or need more. They choose which item has more value to them.

People do not always place a higher value on things that cost more. Even if an item costs more, it might not have a high value to someone who does not want or need it.

People usually compare things before they decide what to buy.

Suppose a family of four people decides to move to a larger apartment. They have to choose an apartment by deciding what they value most.

The family finds two apartments that everyone likes. Both are similar in size, and they cost the same amount of money to rent. The first apartment is close to the children's school and to the parents' jobs. However, it is far away from the community center and the grocery store. The second apartment is farther away from their school and jobs. However, it is closer to the community center and grocery store.

How would the family choose which apartment to rent? They would decide which they value more, being closer to their school and jobs or to the community center and grocery store.

This family chose the first apartment. They decided that it was more important to be closer to their school and jobs. They spend more time either going to school or working. Therefore, the first apartment has more value to them.

4. **Underline** the sentence that tells why the family chose the first apartment.

Choices in Communities

People living in communities around the world make choices every day. That is because no one can have everything. People have to decide what has value to them.

Often, people in a community work together to make choices. In this way, most people's needs can be met.

For example, imagine that two communities have a scarcity of money. People living in both communities decide that they can save money by working together. The communities decide to have one police department for both communities instead of one for each. This plan helps everyone stay safe and saves money.

People around the world make choices when they spend money.

World communities can help each other make choices, too. For example, one country might have a scarcity of water and another might have an abundance. People from both countries could meet and decide how much water they have together. Then, they could make a plan to share their water. This plan makes sure everyone has enough.

5. Suppose your community's playground has a scarcity of baseball supplies. **Describe** a way you can work with others to get the supplies people want.

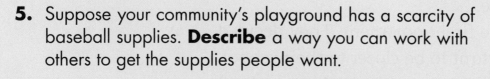

6. ◉ **Main Idea and Details** Suppose you are going camping. **Fill in** the chart by listing your needs and wants. **Tell** whether each item is a need or a want.

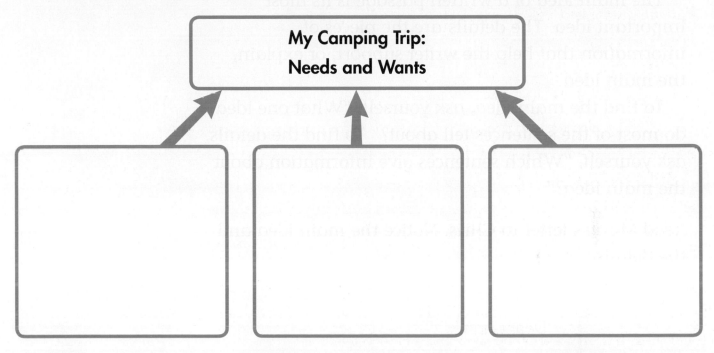

My Camping Trip:
Needs and Wants

7. ? **Write** about a time you had to choose between getting something you needed and something you wanted. **Explain** why you made the choice you did.

my Story Ideas

....

....

....

....

■ **Stop!** I need help with ....

❙❙ **Wait!** I have a question about ....

▶ **Go!** Now I know ....

Main Idea and Details

The main idea of a written passage is its most important idea. The details are the pieces of information that help the writer support, or explain, the main idea.

To find the main idea, ask yourself, "What one idea do most of the sentences tell about?" To find the details, ask yourself, "Which sentences give information about the main idea?"

Read Maria's letter to Chris. Notice the main idea and the details.

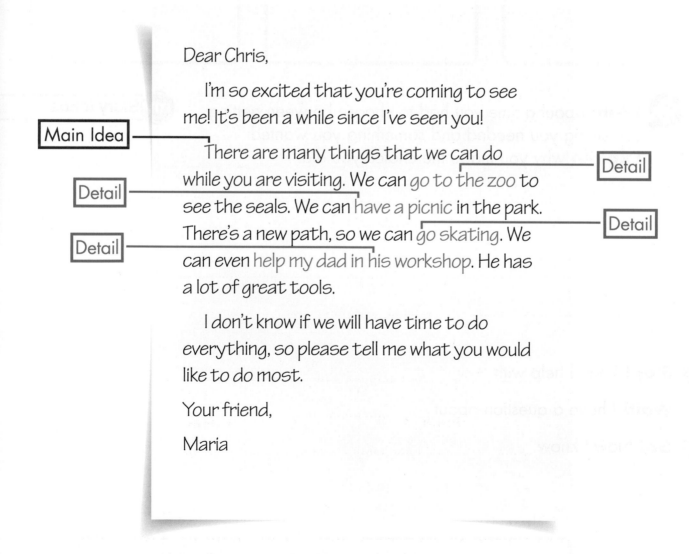

Dear Chris,

I'm so excited that you're coming to see me! It's been a while since I've seen you!

Main Idea — There are many things that we can do while you are visiting. **Detail** — We can *go to the zoo* to see the seals. We can *have a picnic* in the park. There's a new path, so we can *go skating*. We can even *help my dad in his workshop*. He has a lot of great tools. **Detail** **Detail** **Detail**

I don't know if we will have time to do everything, so please tell me what you would like to do most.

Your friend,

Maria

I will know how to find the main idea and details in a written passage.

Read Chris's letter to Maria. Then **answer** the question.

> Dear Maria,
>
> Wow! It's hard to choose from so many great ideas.
>
> I think I would like to go to the zoo with you. I'd love to see the seals. Mom says your zoo has a lot of them. I'd also like to see the pandas. We don't have pandas in our zoo. Maybe we can have a picnic there, too. I'm sure they have picnic tables.
>
> I can't wait to see you again!
>
> Your friend,
> Chris

Fill in the chart below with the main idea and details from Chris's letter to Maria.

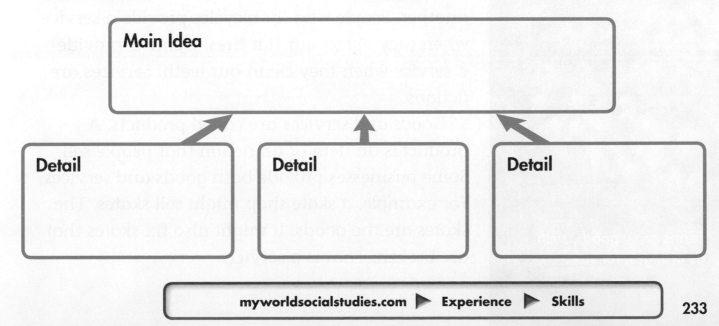

Producers and Consumers

Envision It!

Write a caption that describes what is happening in the picture.

Farms grow goods, such as oranges, for sale.

Your community has many businesses, both large and small. Some businesses make things, such as sneakers or computers. Other businesses sell these things. Some businesses do things for people, such as repair cars or clean clothes.

All businesses try to provide what people need or want. Let's look at how some businesses work.

Goods and Services

Goods are things that people make or grow and then sell. Sneakers and computers are examples of goods that are made. Oranges and other crops are goods that are grown.

A **service** is work that one person does for another. People who fix bicycles provide a service when they repair our flat tires. Dentists provide a service when they clean our teeth. Services are actions.

Goods and services are called products. A product is an item or an action that people sell. Some businesses provide both goods and services. For example, a skate shop might sell skates. The skates are the goods. It might also fix skates that are broken. That is a service.

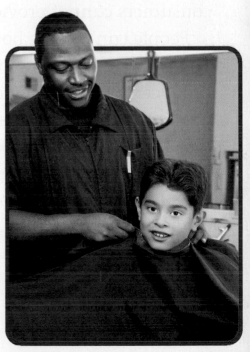
UNLOCK THE BIG ?

I will know the difference between goods and services and between producers and consumers.

Vocabulary

goods
service
producer
consumer

human resource
capital resource
profit

What are some goods and services that are available in your community? You might have a grocery store on your block that sells fruits, vegetables, bread, and milk. These foods are the store's goods.

Hair salons often sell both goods and services. Many salons sell goods, such as shampoo and hairbrushes. They also sell haircuts. Because it is an action, cutting hair is a service.

1. ◎ **Main Idea and Details Fill in** the chart with three goods and three services.

Goods	Services
....	....
....	....
....	....
....	....
....	....
....	....

A hair salon offers services such as haircutting.

Producers and Consumers

Few people can make all of the products and services they need and want. Instead, most people buy goods and services from other people or from stores and businesses.

A person who makes a product or provides a service is called a **producer.** If you have ever made something, such as a birthday card, you have been a producer.

When people spend money to buy things they need or want, they are called **consumers.** If you have ever bought something, such as an apple, you have been a consumer. Consumers buy goods and services. The study of how goods and services are produced, distributed, and consumed is called economics.

This producer is making a wooden chair.

Producers and consumers need each other. Producers need consumers to buy the goods they create and the services they offer. Consumers need producers to offer the goods and services that consumers cannot provide for themselves.

People can also be both producers and consumers. The man in the picture who is making a chair is a producer. He is making a product that someone else will buy. He is a consumer, too. That is because he bought the wood and tools from someone who produced them.

Consumers buy goods from people, not just from stores.

2. **Look** at the picture. **Circle** the producer.

236

Resources All Around Us

Suppose you need help hanging a poster on your wall. If you ask your friend to hold up the poster while you tape it, you are using your friend as a human resource. A **human resource** is a person who makes products or provides services. Human resources can also be called producers.

There are many other kinds of resources. Natural resources are useful materials that come from the earth. Many kinds of natural resources are needed to make goods. Water, soil, and wood are all natural resources.

Capital resources are the things needed to produce goods and services. Computers, tools, and money are all capital resources.

Businesses try to use their resources wisely. When they do, they might make a profit. A **profit** is the money that businesses have left after their costs are paid.

What are these costs? Businesses pay their workers, or human resources, money for doing their jobs. Some businesses buy goods to make the products they sell. Businesses also pay for the heat and water they use. In addition, businesses pay for their capital resources. These include the machines they use to make their products.

3. List the three types of resources that people and businesses use.

....

....

....

This doctor and nurse are human resources.

Changing Roles

Suppose you are making lemonade on a hot day. You are a producer because you are making something. The good you are making is lemonade.

You are a consumer, too. That is because you had to buy things to make the lemonade. You probably bought lemons, sugar, and cups.

Producers and consumers can change roles. For example, bicycle factories are producers because they make bicycles that people buy.

However, they are consumers, too. That is because they probably buy some of the things they use to make bicycles. They may not make the tires or the paint they use. Instead, they may buy these things from tire stores and paint stores. That makes them consumers of tires and paint.

The factories use these items to make bicycles that they sell to consumers. Consumers pay money for the bicycles. The bicycle factory can then use this money to make more bicycles. Producers and consumers often change roles in the process of buying and selling products.

People can be both producers and consumers.

4. **Write** one sentence that describes a time when you were a producer. **Write** one sentence that describes a time when you were a consumer.

....

....

....

5. ⊙ **Main Idea and Details Explain** what producers and consumers are. Then **write** about how they help each other.

a. Producers are

....

....

b. Consumers are

....

....

c. How do producers and consumers help each other?

....

....

....

....

6. ❓ **Write** about a service that you can perform for someone in your family or in your neighborhood.

my Story Ideas

....

....

....

■ **Stop!** I need help with ....

❚❚ **Wait!** I have a question about ....

▶ **Go!** Now I know ....

Exchanging Goods and Services

Describe what you think the boy and girl are doing in this picture.

Fruits, like these mangoes, are goods you can buy.

COSTA RICA MANGO $ 1 EACH

Have you ever wondered how fruit gets to a store? The farmer who grew the fruit probably met with a worker from the store. The store worker, or the buyer, looked at the fruit. The farmer, or the seller, talked about why the fruit was worth buying.

Then the buyer and the seller talked about the price. When they agreed, they made a deal. The store worker gave money to the farmer in exchange for the fruit. Finally, the fruit was delivered to the store. That is how fruit gets to a store.

Trade and Barter

Communities in the United States and around the world depend on each other for many things. One thing they need to do is trade with each other. When people **trade,** they use money to buy and sell goods and services. However, when they **barter,** they do not use money. Instead, one person gives a good or a service to another in exchange for a different good or service.

People have been trading and bartering goods for thousands of years. People in one place often make just a few goods. Then they barter their goods with people who have goods they need.

Vocabulary

trade	free market
barter	import
supply	export
demand	

Bartering can be useful when people from different cultures meet. When Europeans came to the Americas, for example, they could not use money from their home countries. So they bartered with Native Americans to get things they needed.

Europeans gave the Native Americans tools and animals, such as axes and horses. In return, the Native Americans gave the Europeans food, such as corn and potatoes, and furs that the Europeans used to stay warm.

Today, people usually use money to get the goods and services they need. Money makes trading goods and services easier. That is because money has a value that everyone agrees on. Money is very light, so it is portable, or easy to carry. It can also be divided into smaller units. If you buy something that costs 50 cents with a one dollar bill, the seller can give you 50 cents in change. Money is also durable, which means it can last a long time.

1. **⊙ Compare and Contrast Underline** the text that tells how trading and bartering are different.

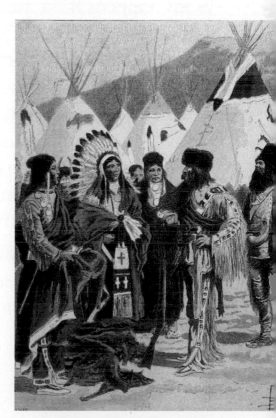

At first, people bartered for goods.

Supply and Demand

The amount of goods or services that people can sell is called the **supply**. The amount of goods or services that people want and can buy is called the **demand**.

In most cases, if the supply of something goes up, the price goes down. Suppose a store owner has too many sweaters. The owner may lower the price of the sweaters. As a result, more shoppers might buy them.

Many things might cause the supply of sweaters to go down. If there are few sheep, there might not be much wool to make sweaters. If there is a storm, trucks might not be able to bring the sweaters to a store.

What happens if the supply goes down? The price might go up. Some people might decide to pay a higher price because they really want a sweater.

Many things might cause the demand for sweaters to go down. If the weather is warm, people might not want them. If few people buy sweaters, the price might go down.

Prices often depend on the size of the supply. If there is too much of something, prices often go down.

2. ◉ **Cause and Effect Choose** a good or service you use. Then **write** about what might cause the supply of that good or service to go down.

....

....

....

....

242

Moving Goods Around the World

Today, people around the world trade easily. That is because they can move goods from one country to another in only a few days.

Fruit spoils very fast. However, different types of transportation, such as airplanes, trains, ships, and trucks, can bring fruit to stores quickly. This means people can buy fresh fruit grown far away that still tastes good.

As people keep buying fruit, the supply goes down. But that amount can rise again quickly. That is because trucks and ships can bring more fruit to the store.

Packing goods into big containers like these makes it easy to ship goods around the world quickly.

Communication also helps people today to trade quickly. People use the Internet and telephones to communicate instantly. They order products online or by phone. In this way, transportation and communication together help the supply of products to rise quickly.

3. **Explain** what helps the supply of products to rise quickly today.

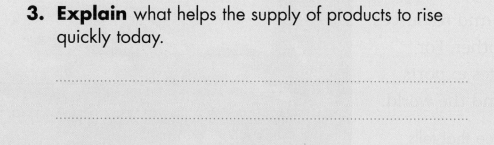

Free Market

In the United States, people and companies do business in a free market. A **free market** allows people to choose what to make and what to buy.

Farmers in a free market decide which crops to plant. Factories decide which goods to make. Store owners decide which products to sell. People decide which goods and services they want to buy.

Some countries do not have a free market. In these countries, the government controls what is bought and sold.

The United States imports olive oil from Italy.

Worldwide Trade

Today, people around the world buy and sell goods and services to one another. Trade between countries is called international trade.

People and countries import products from other countries. To **import** means to bring products and resources into one country from another. For example, the United States imports wool from Australia and New Zealand. Oil is imported to the United States from Russia and Saudi Arabia.

People and countries also export products to other countries. To **export** means to send products and resources from one country to another. For example, the United States exports cotton to countries around the world.

4. **Underline** the sentence that tells what happens when countries do not have a free market.

Korea exports cars to the United States.

244

5. 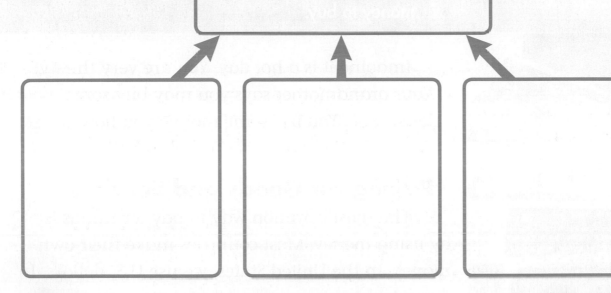 **Main Idea and Details Fill in** the chart with details that support the main idea.

> Today, people exchange goods and services by trading.

6. **Write** about how you exchanged a good or a service with a friend or a family member.

my Story Ideas

....

....

Stop! I need help with ....

Wait! I have a question about ....

Go! Now I know ....

Spending and Saving

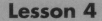

Envision It!

Write what you think the girl might be saving her money to buy.

People in the United States, Japan, and Mexico use different forms of money. In Japan, people use yen.

Imagine it is a hot day. You are very thirsty! Your grandmother says you may buy some lemonade. You use some money you have saved. Suddenly, the day does not feel so hot!

Paying for Goods and Services

The most common way to pay for things is by using money. Most countries make their own money. In the United States, we use U.S. dollars. In Canada, people use Canadian dollars. In Mexico, people use pesos. People in the islands of the Caribbean use various forms of money. Some, like people in Jamaica, use dollars. In Haiti, people use gourdes. In Aruba, people use florin.

Instead of using money, people can also pay for things by bartering, or exchanging one thing for another. For example, you might give your cousin your granola bar in exchange for his apple.

Credit is another way to pay for things. **Credit** is a promise to pay for something. A **credit card** lets the cardholder buy things and pay for them later. The cardholder pays the credit card company every month until all of the money is paid back.

I will know different ways people pay for goods and services and how they save money.

Vocabulary

credit	interest
credit card	deposit
savings	loan
bank	budget

Savings

The money a person earns but does not spend is called that person's **savings.** For example, suppose you walk a neighbor's dog for a week. You earn $5, but you buy a comic book for $2. If you subtract $2 from $5, you have $3 left. Your leftover $3 is money you can save to use later.

People usually save money over a period of weeks, months, or even years. In this way, they can plan to buy something that they need or want. You can save money for small things, such as a basketball or a special jacket. You can also save for more expensive things, like a summer vacation or a college education. It takes longer to save for something that costs a lot of money than for something that only costs a few dollars.

1. **Write** two ways people can pay for things they want and need.

....

....

Doing small jobs for your neighbors can help you save money.

People can save money by putting it into a bank.

Savings Accounts in Banks

You can save money at home in a small jar or container. You can also save outside your home at a bank. A **bank** is a business that keeps, exchanges, and lends money to people.

A bank is a good place to save money because banks give you a bonus for saving. This bonus is called interest. **Interest** is the money a bank gives you for letting it hold your money. The bank gives you money while you save, and interest makes your savings grow.

Here is how a bank works. The money you put in the bank is called a **deposit.** The banker counts the money you deposit and records the amount in a little book or on a small piece of paper. Some banks also let you check your deposits online.

You might deposit your money by handing it to a banker or by using a cash machine. Either way, banks help you save. They keep your money safe, and they give you interest for saving.

2. ⦿ **Main Idea and Details Fill in** the chart with three details that support the main idea.

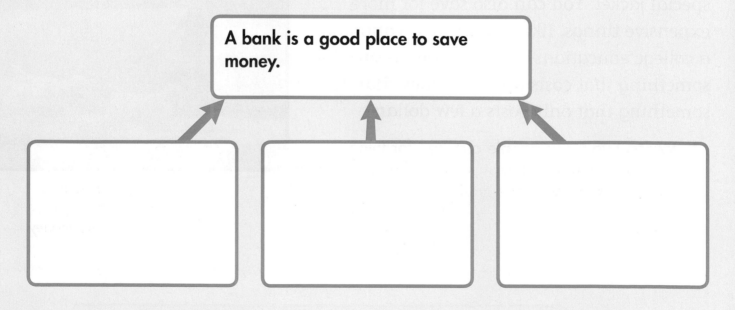

A bank is a good place to save money.

Borrowing Money

Sometimes people have to buy something, but they do not have enough money saved to pay for it. In these cases, they might need to borrow money from a person or from a bank.

When banks lend money, the money is called a **loan.** Where do banks get the money to lend to people? Banks lend the money that other people are saving. That is why banks pay interest. They pay people who save in exchange for using their money.

A loan is not a gift. People must pay it back. They have to pay a fee to borrow the money. That fee is also called interest. Read the chart below to see the steps involved in getting a loan.

How to Get a Loan

1. A person talks to a loan officer at the bank.

⬇

2. The bank decides how much money it will lend.

⬇

3. The bank makes sure the person is able to pay back the loan.

⬇

4. The person signs papers that tell how much the bank is lending and when the loan must be paid back.

⬇

5. The person gets the money. Soon, he or she starts paying back the loan and the interest.

3. Underline the sentence that tells where banks get the money they lend to people.

Personal Budgets

Making a budget is a good way to help you save and spend your money. A **budget** is a plan that shows your income, expenses, and savings. Your income is the money you earn. Your expenses are what you spend. It is wise to list the money you want to save.

A budget helps you keep track of your money. You can also use a budget to save for special items. For example, Sue wants to buy a backpack that costs $25. She also needs $10 to buy her mother a birthday gift. She finds a job delivering newspapers that pays $18 each week to help her save money.

Sue makes a budget to figure out how long she will have to work in order to save enough money to buy the backpack and the gift. After three weeks, she has enough money for both things she wants to buy.

MY BUDGET			
Week	Income	Expenses	Savings
1	$18	$6	$12
2	$18	$2	$16
3	$18	$10	$8

Budgets help people plan how to use their money.

Community Budgets

Communities have budgets just like people do. The mayor of a city might make a budget that helps the community buy new police cars. The city council might make a budget that helps it plan how it will pay to fix the town pool. The school board might make a budget that helps it buy new books. They must all plan how to use the money they get from taxes to buy what the community needs and wants.

4. ◎ **Compare and Contrast Explain** how personal and community budgets are different.

....

....

....

5. ◉ **Main Idea and Details Fill in** the chart below with information about how people pay for things.

Ways to Pay for Things	How It Works	Why It Is Useful
Money		
Barter		
Credit		
Loan		

6. ❓ **Write** about two ways you can save money.

my Story Ideas

....

....

....

🔲 **Stop!** I need help with ....

⏸ **Wait!** I have a question about ....

▶ **Go!** Now I know ....

Graph Skills

Line Graphs

Graphs show information in pictures. A line graph is a graph that shows how something changes over time. Follow the steps below to read a line graph.

1. Read the title at the top of the graph to learn what the graph shows. Then look at the numbers along the left side of the graph. In the graph below, they tell how many skateboards were sold. Look at the words along the bottom of the graph. In this graph, they tell in which month the total was calculated.

2. Each dot on a line graph shows an amount at a certain point in time. Put your finger on the second dot from the left. Move your finger to the left on the light blue line until you reach a number. The number is 10. Move your finger back to the dot. Now move your finger down on the light blue line until you reach a month. The month is April. This dot shows that 10 skateboards were sold by the end of April.

3. Each dot shows the total number of skateboards that were sold. Follow the line to see how the number of skateboards sold changed over time.

Read the line graph below. Then **answer** the questions.

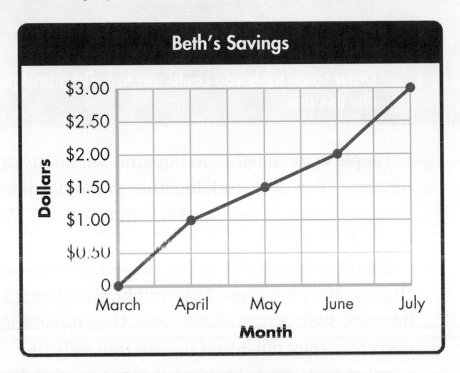

Beth's Savings

1. **Write** how much money Beth had in March.

   ....

2. In April, Beth had $1.00. **Look** at how much money Beth had in May. Then **write** how much money Beth saved between April and May.

   ....

3. **Write** how much money Beth saved by July.

   ....

4. **Explain** what this line graph shows.

   ....

   ....

Many Different Jobs

Draw some tools you could use to build a bridge like this one.

Careful planning makes a project successful.

People work together to buy and sell goods and services. They also work together to build things. Suppose a new playground is being planned. What would be needed?

People might decide to put new sand and wood chips in the play area. They might also decide to buy new swings and slides. Once they make these decisions, they must find a store that sells the supplies they need. They must also hire people to do the work.

Planning for a Job

People in a town have been talking about how difficult it is to get across a river. They have to walk or drive a long way to reach the bridge. They ask the local government to build a new bridge, and the government agrees. However, the workers cannot just start building. First, they need to think about the whole project.

They must ask many questions, including Where should the bridge be built? What type of bridge will be best? How much will the bridge cost? What are the laws about bridges? Once they have answers to these questions, they can create a plan.

I will know how to describe how specialization and division of labor help people make products.

Vocabulary

specialization
division of labor
interdependence

Once they have a plan, the workers must gather the resources they need to complete the job. They need human resources, including people who can plan and build the bridge. They also need people who can measure distances, work with special tools, and use heavy machines.

They need natural resources, too, such as soil and wood. Most importantly, they need open land on both sides of the river so they can build roads that lead on and off the bridge.

In addition, they need capital resources, such as tools, machines, and money. The money is needed to pay the workers and to buy tools, machines, and other supplies.

1. ◉ **Sequence List** three steps involved in planning for a job.

....

....

....

Some projects need natural resources, such as this wood.

Special Skills and Jobs

Projects, like building a bridge, can include many different kinds of jobs. One person might draw the plans for the project, while another might figure out how much it will cost. A third person might get the tools and machines.

Drawing plans for a job is a kind of specialization.

When each person has a special skill and does one job or one part of a project, it is called **specialization.** Specialization leads to a division of labor.

When there is a **division of labor**, a project is divided, or broken down, into smaller jobs. Each person then works on his or her own job, and together they get the project done.

With specialization and division of labor, people do not have to learn every skill needed to complete a job. Instead, they can learn to do one job well. This saves time and money during a project. It also helps a project run smoothly.

Think about how many people it takes to produce the food we eat. Farmers grow crops. They specialize in keeping soil and plants healthy. Factory workers put soup, tuna, and other foods in cans. They specialize in keeping food safe and making it available to many people. Both the farmers and the factory workers have an important role in producing the food we eat.

2. ◉ **Main Idea and Details Explain** why specialization and division of labor are important to a project.

....

....

....

256

Jobs Help the World

Specialization and division of labor help people in communities around the world. That is because people can sell their products and skills to others who need them. Writing, welding, and teaching are skills. Growing food and fixing things are also skills.

People in different countries often develop skills that are important where they live. For example, people who live in places that have many trees might learn to work with wood. People who live in places that have a lot of water might learn to build boats. The people who work with wood sell it to the people who build boats. When these people trade with each other, they all get what they need.

This is why buyers and sellers around the world exchange goods and services. They depend on each other. When people depend on each other to get the things they need and want, it is called **interdependence.**

Trade is not the only way people around the world are interdependent. People attend schools in different countries. They also work in different countries. As they live and work together, people around the world learn from one another. They also better understand others' ideas.

3. Write one way people around the world are interdependent.

....

....

Teaching is a specialized job.

Welding is a specialized job, too.

257

Jobs Today and Long Ago

Just as communities change over time, so do the ways people do their jobs. Long ago, farmers grew all of the food their families ate. They did their work by hand. They bartered for goods they could not make or grow. They grew as much food as they could.

Today, farmers still grow as much food as they can. However, they grow much more than farmers did long ago. That is because many specialize. They also use science to test their soil and add exactly what each crop needs. Machines, such as the harvester shown below, help them work more land.

Many people today have other types of specialized jobs. Some run businesses. Some learn a craft, like carpentry. Others learn to operate special machines.

You have a job, too. Your job is to be a student. You are learning many subjects. You are learning how to work with others and solve problems. You are doing projects in groups. All of these skills will help you become a successful student.

Some of the work that farmers once did by hand is now done by machines.

4. ⊙ **Compare and Contrast Fill in** the diagram to compare and contrast farming long ago and today.

Farming Long Ago **Farming Today**

Both

Got it?

5. ⊙ **Main Idea and Details Explain** what specialization means. Then **write** about how two people in your school specialize in their work.

a. Specialization means

....

b. Two people in my school who specialize are

....

....

6. ❓ **Write** about how you use division of labor at home.

....

....

⬛ **Stop!** I need help with ....

⏸ **Wait!** I have a question about ....

▶ **Go!** Now I know ....

Review and Assessment

Lesson 1

Meeting Our Needs and Wants

1. **Read** the list of items below. **Circle** the items that are needs. **Underline** the items that are wants.

shelter	food	movie ticket
basketball	game	clothing
parrot	water	book

2. **Fill in** the circle next to the correct answer.

   Which of the following means "the value of something you give up when you choose one thing instead of another"?

   ○ scarcity

   ○ abundance

   ○ opportunity cost

   ○ money

Lesson 2

Producers and Consumers

3. **Explain** how you could be both a producer and a consumer.

   ....

   ....

   ....

Review and Assessment

Lesson 3

Exchanging Goods and Services

4. **Fill in** the circle next to the correct answer.

   What happens most of the time when the supply of something goes down?

   ○ The price goes down.

   ○ The price goes up.

   ○ The price stays the same.

   ○ The price keeps changing.

5. ⊙ **Main Idea and Details Write** two details that support the main idea.

   Main Idea: There are two main ways countries trade products.

   Details:

   ....

   ....

   ....

Lesson 4

Spending and Saving

6. **Describe** what people can do to make spending and saving easier.

   ....

   ....

   ....

Lesson 5

Many Different Jobs

7. Write about how the members of a family can use specialization to get things done in their home.

....

....

....

....

....

8. Draw a picture of how you and a partner could clean up your classroom by using division of labor.

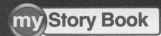

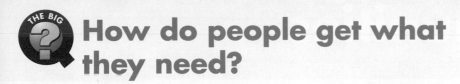
Go online to write and illustrate your own **myStory Book** using the **myStory Ideas** from this chapter.

How do people get what they need?

Everyone has needs and wants. People often need to buy things to meet these needs and wants. Before they buy something, they have to make choices. They often have to work with others to get what they need.

Think about a time you bought a good or a service. **Write** about what you bought and how you made your choice.

....

....

....

Draw a picture showing people working together as producers to make something your community needs.

While you're online, check out the **myStory Current Events** area where you can create your own book on a topic that's in the news.

Celebrating Our Communities

THE BIG ? How is culture shared?

Describe what you like to eat, what you like to wear, and what you like to do in your community.

....

....

....

....

....

Joseph Bruchac
Storyteller

my Story Video

When Joseph Bruchac was a boy, he lived with his grandparents in the mountains of New York. His grandmother had a lot of books all over the house. His grandfather was an Abenaki [ab uh NAK ee] Native American. He taught Bruchac how to explore the woods and how to fish. Bruchac's grandfather never got angry with Joseph when he made a mistake. Instead, his grandfather would talk to him and help him learn from his mistakes. Later, Bruchac learned that this way of teaching was an important part of the Abenaki way of life.

Bruchac's grandparents owned a local store called Bowman's. Bruchac helped his grandparents in the store whenever he could. In winter, he sat by the wood stove and listened as farmers and other customers told stories. Bruchac grew to love books and storytelling. He also loved to write his own stories. As a child, he wrote poems.

Joseph Bruchac named one of his books Bowman's Store, after his grandparents' store.

Joseph Bruchac and Chinua Achebe talked of writing about their cultures.

Bruchac listened to others tell stories about the Abenaki.

When Bruchac was older, he met a writer from Nigeria, a country in Africa, named Chinua Achebe [CHIN wah ah CHAY bay]. Achebe told Bruchac that he had become a writer so he could tell the story of his people, the Igbo. Achebe had read stories about the Igbo that were written by people who did not understand Igbo culture. Achebe wanted to tell the world about his culture from the point of view of his people.

Bruchac understood Achebe's feelings. He heard stories about his own people, the Abenaki, when he visited Abenaki friends and family. Bruchac began to record the stories that were important to him and to the Abenaki culture.

Stories and storytelling are important parts of the Abenaki way of life. Stories are told not just to entertain people, but to teach them. Listeners learn that it is important to treat others kindly, to care for plants and animals, and to share.

Joseph Bruchac brings Abenaki stories and songs to schoolchildren.

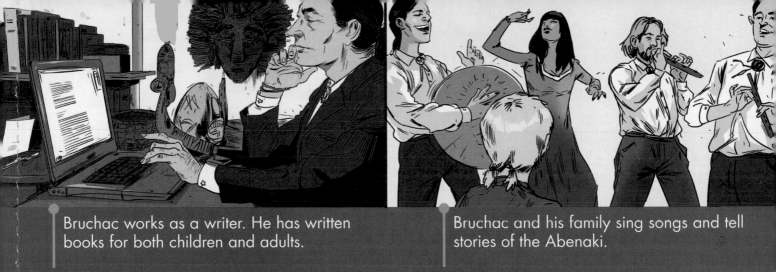

Bruchac works as a writer. He has written books for both children and adults.

Bruchac and his family sing songs and tell stories of the Abenaki.

Stories are also used to teach children how to behave. The Abenaki people do not speak harshly to their children. Instead, if a child misbehaves, the child is told a story to show them the correct way to act. Some stories involve a raccoon that is known to misbehave. Others are about a wise leader. To the Abenaki people, telling stories is the best way to teach. Bruchac explains it this way:

> "A story stays in a child's heart and helps that child grow up straight and strong."

Today, Bruchac lives in the same house in New York in which he grew up. He has written more than 70 books, and he travels around the world as a storyteller. Bruchac also plays music. He, his sister, and his two sons formed a music group called the Dawnland Singers. Together, they play music and tell stories of the Abenaki people.

Think About It Based on this story, why do you think the Abenaki use storytelling as a way to teach others about their culture? As you read the chapter ahead, think about why it was important to Joseph Bruchac to share his culture.

People and Cultures

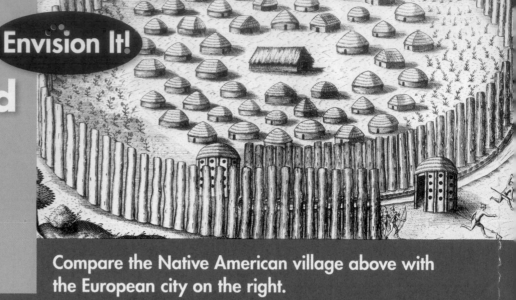

Compare the Native American village above with the European city on the right.

Today, the United States is a nation of many different cultures. Culture includes the language people speak, the religion they follow, the holidays they celebrate, the clothing they wear, and the foods they eat. People who share a similar culture often live near each other in a **cultural region**. There are many different cultural regions in the United States.

Cultural Regions

Every cultural region is shaped by the people who first settled there. For example, Native American groups lived in North America and South America long ago. Then in the 1400s and 1500s, European explorers from Spain, France, and England arrived. They brought their own cultures to the lands they explored. Their cultures were very different from the cultures of the Native Americans they met.

Settlements in North America, 1700–1750

0 800 mi
0 800 km

St. Lawrence River
New France
Nez Percé
Mandan
Iroquois
Mississippi River
Miami
Pomo Shosone
New Spain Hopi
Pawnee
Louisiana
Thirteen Colonies
Navajo
Comanche
Rio Grande
Calusa
ATLANTIC OCEAN
Gulf of Mexico
Caribbean Sea

N E W S

KEY
English
French
Spanish
Hopi Native American group

Vocabulary

cultural region
recreation

Circle the homes in both places. Discuss how they are different.

Soon, more Europeans came to settle the new lands the explorers had found. The map shows where in North America the Europeans settled. The European settlers and the Native Americans often lived near one another. Both groups learned about each other's cultures. For example, in Jamestown, Virginia, the Native Americans taught English settlers new ways to plant crops. The English settlers taught the Native Americans to use the tools that the settlers had brought with them.

Many places throughout North America and South America were once settled by Europeans hundreds of years ago. These places have kept some of the culture that the Europeans brought.

1. **Explain** how the Native Americans helped the English settlers in Jamestown, Virginia.

....

....

....

The Spanish brought building styles, such as these in Toledo, Spain, with them from Europe.

People often use the Caribbean Sea for fishing. Fish are a valuable natural resource in the Caribbean.

Cultures in Warm and Cold Climates

Did you know that climate shapes a cultural region? Climate affects the type of shelters people build, their forms of recreation, the foods they eat, and the clothing they wear. **Recreation** is a way of enjoying yourself.

People who live in warm climates, such as the tropical climate in Central America, often build shelters that help them to stay cool. They may build houses in shaded areas or with powerful air conditioners. In a cold climate, people's homes are built to hold in the heat. They may also have large windows to let in sunlight.

Climate also affects recreation. People who live in warm climates near water can swim, fish, or go boating many months of the year. In cold climates, the water may be frozen for many months.

Fishing in cold climates is not always easy. These children are ice-fishing on a frozen lake in Vermont.

What you eat for dinner tonight may also depend on climate. For example, if you live near rich soil in a temperate climate, you might be able to grow your own vegetables and fruits. If you live near the coast, you might eat some fresh fish. Today, foods from all over the world can be brought to an area by planes, ships, or trucks. However, many people still eat the foods that can be grown or found in their own region.

Climate also helps people choose what kind of clothing to wear. In the warm climates of the southeastern United States, people wear light clothing. These may include shorts and short-sleeved shirts, and hats to protect their skin from the sun. People also wear sandals to help their feet stay cool.

In cold climates, such as in parts of Canada, people need to stay warm. They wear layers of clothes under heavy coats. They wear gloves on their hands and thick hats to keep their heads warm. Places in cold climates are often wet with snow. People wear boots that keep their feet warm and dry.

2. **Write** three ways that climate affects a cultural region.

....

....

In Mexico, people make and sell clothing to wear in the warm climate there.

Climates and World Cultures

The climates in Tibet and Egypt affect the cultures of their people. Tibet is a cultural region in Asia. Egypt is a country in Africa. The climate of Tibet is mostly cold and can be dry. In Egypt, the climate is warm and dry. In fact, Egypt receives less rain than any country in the world!

The people in Tibet live on a plateau. One of the mountains surrounding the plateau is Mount Everest, the tallest mountain in the world! Grasslands cover much of the plateau. Many people in Tibet raise animals, including sheep and yaks. They use the animals in many different ways. They eat cheese and butter made from the milk these animals produce. In some places, people live in tents made from the thick hair of yaks. The yaks' thick hair helps keep the tents warm inside.

Tibet

In Egypt, most people live near the Nile River so they can get water for drinking, bathing, and watering crops. Since much of the land is desert, those who do not live near the river often still rely on it for water. These people may farm by bringing water in from the Nile River or raise animals such as goats, sheep, or camels. Many people build homes with bricks made from the nearby resources of mud and straw. On hot nights people sleep on the flat rooftops to stay cool.

Egypt

3. ⊙ **Compare and Contrast Explain** one way the cultures in Tibet and Egypt are the same and one way the cultures are different.

....

....

....

....

4. ⊙ **Compare and Contrast Fill in** the chart with examples of clothing, recreation, and shelter that can be found in warm climates and cold climates.

	Warm Climate	Cold Climate
Clothing		
Recreation		
Shelter		

5. ？ **Write** whether you live in a cold climate or a warm climate. Then **describe** what you like about how the climate affects your way of life.

my Story Ideas

....

....

⬛ **Stop!** I need help with ....

⏸ **Wait!** I have a question about ....

▶ **Go!** Now I know ....

Compare and Contrast

When you compare two things, you tell how they are alike. When you contrast two things, you tell how they are different. Writers use words as clues to show what is alike and what is different. Words and phrases such as *both, like, similar to,* or *in common* show things that are alike. Words such as *yet, different, but,* and *however* show things that are different.

You can use a diagram to help you compare and contrast information that you read. Read the paragraph below about Jenn and Owen. Then read the diagram to see what is alike and what is different about them.

> Jenn lives in Florida. Owen lives in Alaska. They both live in the United States, but the climate in each state is very different. Jenn lives in a warm climate. She can wear shorts nearly all year. Owen, however, lives in a cold climate. He wears heavy clothes that keep him warm.

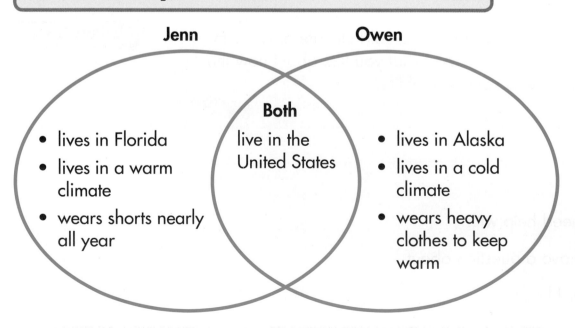

Jenn	Both	Owen
• lives in Florida	live in the United States	• lives in Alaska
• lives in a warm climate		• lives in a cold climate
• wears shorts nearly all year		• wears heavy clothes to keep warm

 **Try it!**

Read about storms that Jenn and Owen have experienced. Then **fill in** the diagram with similarities and differences.

Jenn and Owen have experienced strong storms where they live. In Florida, there are hurricanes. Hurricanes have strong winds and lots of rain. When a hurricane is coming, schools are often closed. Jenn must stay home with her family. They put shutters on the windows to prevent them from breaking. They also stay inside until the hurricane is over.

In Alaska, however, there are blizzards. During a blizzard, there are strong winds and long periods of snowfall. Schools are closed. Before a storm hits, Owen and his family make sure they have lots of wood for the fireplace. Like Jenn, Owen stays home with his family until the storm passes. Blizzards are similar to hurricanes since both storms can cause trees and power lines to fall.

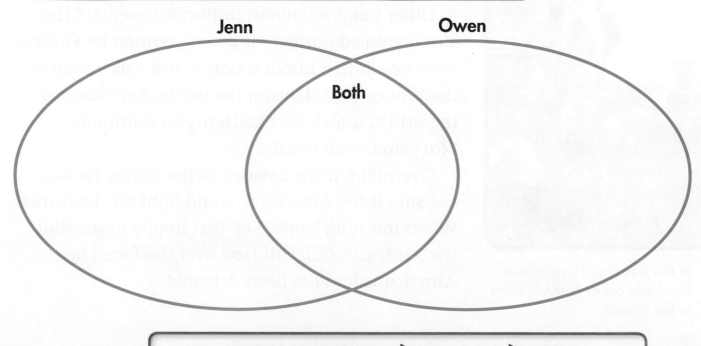

Jenn   Owen

Both

Culture Through the Arts

Envision It!

Write what you see in this painting that shows farm life long ago.

You can learn many things about a culture from the fine art, or the arts, that people create. Most people think of the **arts** as paintings and sculptures, but the arts can also include songs, stories, and dances.

Songs and Culture

People write and sing songs for many different reasons. Some songs are about thoughts and experiences that people have. Songs may also be about a person or a place. They can even include details about the things to see or do in a place.

Other songs tell about important events. "The Star-Spangled Banner" is a song written by Francis Scott Key. It tells about a battle that was fought in the War of 1812. During the battle, Key watched the British attack Fort McHenry in Baltimore, Maryland, with bombs.

Overnight, as he listened to the battle, he was not sure if the Americans could fight off the British. When morning came, Key was happy to see that the American flag still flew over the fort. The Americans had not been defeated.

In this painting, Francis Scott Key looks out at Fort McHenry in the distance.

Vocabulary

arts   hero
anthem   symbol
oral history
folk tale

"The Star-Spangled Banner" became a popular song and in time became the national anthem. An **anthem** is a song of loyalty to a nation. In the song, Key writes how proud he was to see that the American flag was still flying over the fort:

Oh, say can you see by the dawn's early light
What so proudly we hailed at the twilight's last gleaming?
Whose broad stripes and bright stars through the perilous fight,
O'er the ramparts we watched were so gallantly streaming?

All around the world, people celebrate the pride they have for their country when they sing their nation's anthem. National anthems are often sung and played at important events and celebrations.

1. Write why Francis Scott Key wrote "The Star-Spangled Banner."

....

....

In 1931, "The Star-Spangled Banner" became the national anthem of the United States.

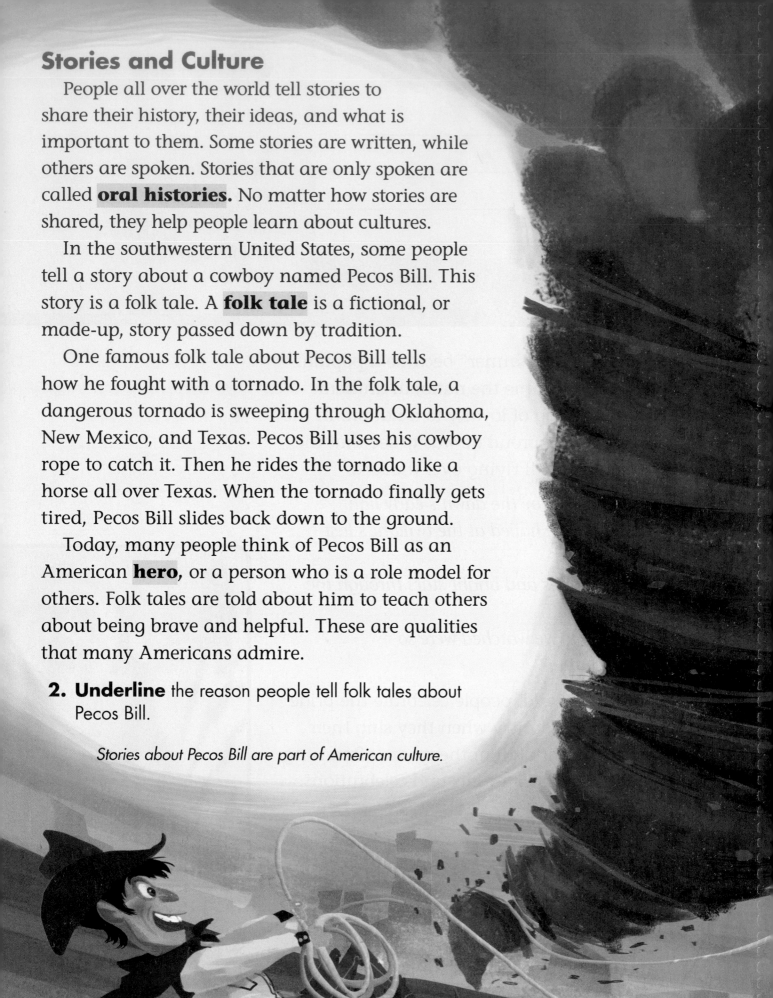

Stories and Culture

People all over the world tell stories to
share their history, their ideas, and what is
important to them. Some stories are written, while
others are spoken. Stories that are only spoken are
called **oral histories.** No matter how stories are
shared, they help people learn about cultures.

In the southwestern United States, some people
tell a story about a cowboy named Pecos Bill. This
story is a folk tale. A **folk tale** is a fictional, or
made-up, story passed down by tradition.

One famous folk tale about Pecos Bill tells
how he fought with a tornado. In the folk tale, a
dangerous tornado is sweeping through Oklahoma,
New Mexico, and Texas. Pecos Bill uses his cowboy
rope to catch it. Then he rides the tornado like a
horse all over Texas. When the tornado finally gets
tired, Pecos Bill slides back down to the ground.

Today, many people think of Pecos Bill as an
American **hero,** or a person who is a role model for
others. Folk tales are told about him to teach others
about being brave and helpful. These are qualities
that many Americans admire.

2. **Underline** the reason people tell folk tales about
   Pecos Bill.

Stories about Pecos Bill are part of American culture.

Sculptures, Paintings, and Culture

Looking at art is another way to learn about different cultures. Some artists use natural resources that are important to their culture to create works of art. They may make clay out of soil or use stone to carve sculptures. In the Black Hills of South Dakota, there is a large mountain. Artists and others are carving the image of Native American leader Crazy Horse into the rock. When the carving is done, it will be more than 600 feet long and about 560 feet tall!

Some artists show details of their culture in paintings. They may also include symbols to help tell a story in their paintings. A **symbol** is a picture that stands for an idea. Artists may show symbols that are important to their country. Some artists in the United States include the American flag or the Statue of Liberty in their paintings.

3. ⊙ **Draw Conclusions Write** why some artists in the United States might include the American flag in their paintings.

....

....

....

....

Crazy Horse Memorial

Childe Hassam, an American artist, shows the American flag in this painting.

Dance and Culture

Dance is an important part of a group's culture. Long ago in Hawaii, a dance called the hula was performed for chiefs, kings, or queens. In a hula dance, the dancers used smooth and flowing movements of their arms and hips. The dancers wore costumes made from local resources that were important to the people. For example, the flowers on the island were made into necklaces called leis. Today, the hula is performed for all people.

Hula dancers

In areas near the Appalachian Mountains in the eastern part of the United States, people do folk dances. Folk dances are dances that have been passed down from one generation to another. Square dancing is a type of folk dance. Dancers stand in a "square." Each side of the square is made up of two people. They listen to a singer who calls out the instructions for each movement. For example, the singer may tell the dancers to move in a circle. There are a variety of movements. The square dancers often do not know what movement they will perform next!

Ballet dancers

In ballet, dancers make smooth movements. They may jump, spin, or dance on their toes. Many ballet dancers wear costumes and pointed shoes. Russian ballet dancers are well known throughout the world. In France and Russia, ballet dancing was first performed only for kings and queens. Today, however, people all over the world can see a ballet performance.

4. **Compare and Contrast Fill in** the diagram to compare the hula dance and ballet.

Hula   **Ballet**

Both

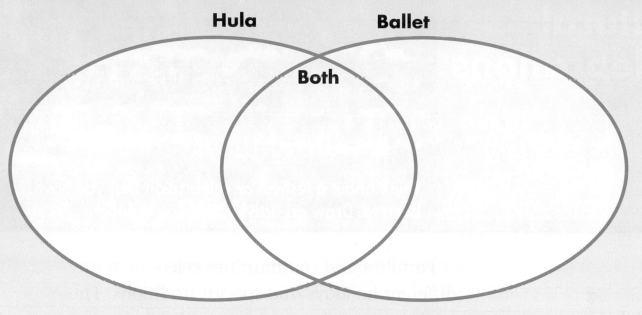

Got it?

5. **Compare and Contrast Think** about each of the arts described in this lesson. Then **explain** how all of the arts are alike.

....

....

....

6. **Describe** some of the arts you can find in your community. **Explain** what they tell about your community's culture.    my Story Ideas

....

....

....

■ **Stop!** I need help with ....

❚❚ **Walt!** I have a question about ....

▶ **Go!** Now I know ....

Cultural Celebrations

Think about a festival or celebration that you have been to. Draw an activity that you did there.

Families and communities celebrate many different holidays and special traditions. These celebrations help people remember important people or events.

Culture Through Traditions

People often have traditions that they follow on holidays. People in a culture learn these traditions from older family members or from people in their community. The traditions are part of the holiday each year.

An Independence Day celebration

Traditions can include eating a certain food, such as turkey on Thanksgiving. Other traditions include certain activities, such as watching fireworks on Independence Day. On some holidays there is a tradition to wear a certain color. On St. Patrick's Day, many people wear the color green.

UNLOCK THE BIG ? I will know how people share their culture through celebrations.

Vocabulary

landmark
harvest

Days to Honor Leaders

Some holidays are held to celebrate and honor people. Martin Luther King Jr. was an important leader. He worked to get African Americans the same civil rights as other Americans. He wanted to bring about change peacefully, without force. People celebrate his life on Martin Luther King Jr. Day, a national holiday in January. People have also created statues to honor him.

King followed the ideas of Mohandas Gandhi from India. Gandhi believed that people should not use violence. He worked for change in his home country of India. He used peaceful ways and did not harm people. People in India celebrate Gandhi's birthday on October 2. On that day, people do not go to school or work. Instead, families do special works of service for others.

1. **◉ Compare and Contrast Underline** sentences that show how Martin Luther King Jr. and Mohandas Gandhi were alike.

This statue of Martin Luther King Jr. is in Texas.

Celebrating Independence

People in the United States celebrate Independence Day on the Fourth of July. Many Americans celebrate this holiday with their family and their friends. They hold parades, gather for picnics, and meet to watch fireworks.

Many symbols and landmarks of the United States are part of Independence Day celebrations. A **landmark** is a building or other structure that is important to a culture. People gather at landmarks such as the Statue of Liberty in New York and the Liberty Bell in Philadelphia. People also wave American flags and fly them in front of their homes and businesses. It is also a tradition to wear red, white, and blue clothing.

Many other countries celebrate a day for independence, as well. In India, people celebrate their independence from British rule on August 15. People fly colorful kites and watch the raising of the Indian flag. The prime minister, or government leader, of India speaks about the many accomplishments made by the Indian people during the year.

People in India celebrate their independence from Great Britain.

Brazil celebrates its independence from Portugal on September 7. Just as people in the United States do, Brazilians celebrate their independence with parades and fireworks. People also fly the flag of Brazil.

In Mexico, there are two celebrations of freedom. On September 16, Mexicans celebrate their independence from Spanish rule. The celebration includes a parade that passes by a memorial statue of Miguel Hidalgo de Costilla. Hidalgo was a Roman Catholic priest whose famous battle cry marked the beginning of the Mexican War of Independence in 1810.

On May 5, people in both Mexico and the United States celebrate Mexico's victory against French troops. This holiday is called Cinco de Mayo, which means "Fifth of May." On Cinco de Mayo people typically watch parades, listen to music, and do or watch dances.

Colorful dresses and Mexican foods are part of many Cinco de Mayo celebrations.

2. **Fill in** the chart below with information about independence celebrations in India and Mexico.

Independence Celebrations

India - August 15	Mexico - May 5

Harvest Celebrations

People in many different cultures celebrate a large harvest. A **harvest** is the crops gathered at the end of the growing season. In the United States, people hold festivals to celebrate corn harvests, cranberry harvests, and even strawberry harvests.

In Japan, a celebration is held in the hopes of a good harvest of rice. During the celebration, rice seedlings are planted in the fields. Throughout the day, people sing and dance to celebrate. Later in the year, another celebration is held to give thanks for the rice harvest.

Some holidays began as harvest celebrations but are now celebrated for other reasons. The first Thanksgiving was a harvest celebration. Settlers from England called Pilgrims gathered with Native Americans to celebrate their harvest and to give thanks. Today, Thanksgiving is in November. Families and friends gather to eat a special meal and celebrate what they are thankful for.

In Japan, people plant rice at a harvest celebration.

Kwanzaa is a celebration that was based on a harvest festival held in some countries in Africa. In the United States and in some countries in Central America, African Americans celebrate Kwanzaa to honor important values.

3. **Underline** the harvest celebrations that take place in the United States.

During Kwanzaa, families light candles and share their values.

Got it?

4. ⊙ **Compare and Contrast Choose** two independence celebrations you read about. **Write** how they are alike, and **explain** how they are different.

....

....

....

....

5. ⍰ **Write** about a cultural celebration that you share with your community.

my Story Ideas

....

....

....

⬜ **Stop!** I need help with ....

⏸ **Wait!** I have a question about ....

▷ **Go!** Now I know ....

Lesson 4

Our Nation's Diversity

Envision It!

Write about what you can learn from your classmates about other cultures.

People from all over the world have come to live in the United States. Some have come to find new jobs. Others have come in search of freedom. Because so many people have come to live in the United States, you can find diversity in each region. If there is **diversity**, that means there are many differences among people. There is diversity at work, in schools, and in communities. This diversity allows people in each region to build friendships with people from other cultures.

Susan From Seattle, Washington

Susan lives with her family in Seattle, Washington, in the West region of the United States. Susan's **ancestors,** or relatives who lived long ago, came to Seattle from the country of Japan. They came to the United States in the 1800s in search of gold. Susan lives in downtown Seattle. She lives in the urban area many people call the International District.

There are people from all over the world living in Seattle.

UNLOCK
THE BIG
?
I will know how people share and express their culture.

Vocabulary
....
diversity
ancestor
pow wow

In the International District there are people from all over the world, including Japan and China. Near her home, Susan shops with her mother for rice and spices from Asia that they use to make traditional Japanese meals. Many of these meals include rice and vegetables.

When Susan is at home, she speaks Japanese with her parents and her grandmother. At school, Susan speaks English like the rest of her classmates. Susan enjoys playing with friends and taking care of her family's garden. One of her favorite places to visit is the Japanese Garden in Seattle. It reminds her of all the cherry trees she saw on her last visit to Japan. In Japan, people celebrate when the cherry trees bloom.

1. **Write** what Susan does to show, or demonstrate, her Japanese culture at home.

....

....

....

Susan reads in the garden.

Charlie From Comanche Nation

Charlie lives in the Southwest region of the United States. Charlie's family are Comanche Native Americans. His ancestors have lived on the same land for hundreds of years. Today, some land in Oklahoma is reserved for the Comanches. This means it will always belong to the Comanches.

Charlie and his family attend gatherings called **pow wows.** At the pow wows, Charlie and his family sing and dance. They meet with other Native Americans to celebrate their cultures.

Manuel From Chicago, Illinois

Manuel is from Chicago, Illinois. Chicago is a city in the Midwest region of the United States. Manuel lives in a part of Chicago where many people from Mexico, Central America, and South America have settled. In Manuel's neighborhood, most people speak Spanish at home.

Manuel's family came from Mexico to Chicago three years ago. They came to start a better life. Today, Manuel has many relatives in his neighborhood. Each Sunday they go to a Catholic church because religion is an important part of their culture.

2. ◎ **Main Idea and Details**
Underline characteristics of Manuel's and Charlie's culture.

Charlie and his family enjoy going to pow wows.

Manuel speaks Spanish with his family, but at school he speaks English.

Sam From Long Island, New York

Sam lives on a farm on Long Island in the Northeast region of the United States. Sam's ancestors came from Italy. They traveled by ship and arrived at Ellis Island in the 1880s. Ellis Island was a center where newcomers came before they could enter the United States. His ancestors moved to Long Island to be farmers. Today, Sam lives on the same farm where his ancestors lived.

Since Sam was first learning to speak, his parents taught him to speak Italian. They want him to be able to speak to their relatives who still live in Italy. They also sing many Italian songs that his parents learned when they were young.

Sam helps his father sell their crops at the local farmers' market.

Eating together is important to Sam's family. On the weekends, they gather in the middle of the day to eat a large meal. Sam's grandmother cooks many different Italian foods. Sam's favorite is ravioli! Sam loves to help his grandmother make and arrange the noodles.

3. ◉ **Compare and Contrast Explain** how Sam's and Charlie's cultures are similar and different.

....

....

....

....

....

Abby From Atlanta, Georgia

Abby lives in Atlanta, in the Southeast region of the United States. Atlanta is the largest city in Georgia. It is also a city with great diversity.

Abby is African American. Her ancestors were brought to Georgia from West Africa. They were forced to work on large farms called plantations with no pay. After the American Civil War, her ancestors were set free and they began to farm their own land.

Today, Abby's father works in the public library. He helps people learn about the history of the city and the history of African Americans. When Abby's father was young, his family began to celebrate Kwanzaa. Today, Abby's family has continued this tradition. During Kwanzaa, Abby likes to discuss the seven symbols and values that are part of the celebration.

4. Write how you know that Abby's ancestors are important to her family.

....

....

....

....

Abby likes to read different types of books at the library.

5. ◉ **Compare and Contrast Review** the information in this lesson about Manuel and Susan. **Fill in** the diagram to compare and contrast their cultures.

Manuel's Mexican Culture   Susan's Japanese Culture

Both

6. ❓ **Describe** one way in which your community shows diversity.

my Story Ideas

....

....

....

....

....

⬛ **Stop!** I need help with ....

⏸ **Wait!** I have a question about ....

▶ **Go!** Now I know ....

Research

When you research a topic, you learn more about it. You can use the information you find to write a paper about what you have learned.

Follow these suggestions as you think about researching a topic.

1. Narrow the topic, or choose one small part of the topic.

2. Decide what kind of information you want to find out about the topic.

3. Choose at least two sources that you can use to find the information you need. You can use print sources, technology sources, or community sources. Look at the chart below to see examples of each type of source.

4. Choose pictures that relate to and show more information about your topic.

This student is using a print source to research a topic.

Sources of Information		
Print Sources	**Technology Sources**	**Community Sources**
book	Internet	community members who provide useful information
dictionary	CD-ROM	history center
atlas	television show	museum
encyclopedia	radio show	
almanac		
magazine article		

Suppose you are researching national holidays. **Answer** the questions below about how you would do your research.

Topic: National Holidays

1. First, you need to narrow the topic. **Write** one national holiday you would like to research.

   ....

2. **Explain** what kind of information you want to find about the holiday.

   ....

   ....

3. **List** two sources you could use to learn about the topic. **Tell** which type of source each one is.

   ....

   ....

4. **Describe** the pictures you would include in a paper about the topic.

   ....

   ....

   ....

5. **Use** the Internet to **find** information about the holiday you chose. **Write** one fact that you find.

   ....

   ....

Lesson 1

People and Cultures

1. **Circle** the picture that shows what a person might use for fun in a cold climate.

Watering can

Surfboard

Sled

Lesson 2

Culture Through the Arts

2. **List** two kinds of art that can help tell about a culture.

....

....

3. **Explain** why many people sing a national anthem.

....

....

4. **Write** two ways that stories are shared. Then **explain** why storytelling is important to a culture.

....

....

....

Lesson 3

Cultural Celebrations

5. **Write** an example of a tradition that people often follow on holidays.

....

....

6. **Explain** how people honor Martin Luther King Jr.

....

....

....

7. ◎ **Compare and Contrast Fill in** the diagram with details that tell the similarities and differences between independence celebrations and harvest celebrations.

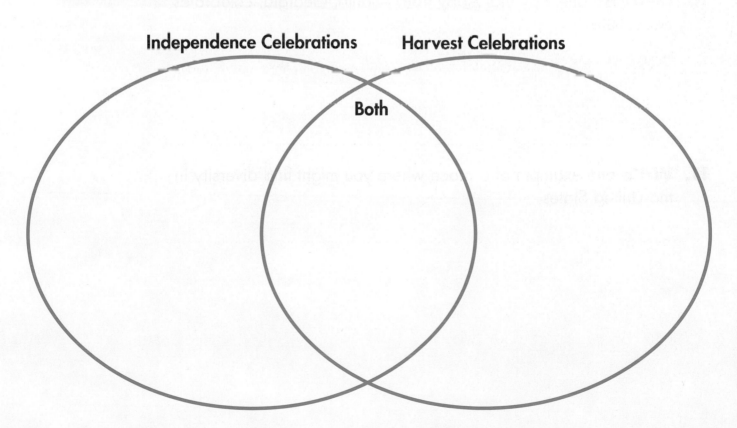

Independence Celebrations   Harvest Celebrations

Both

Lesson 4

Our Nation's Diversity

8. **Fill in** the circle next to the correct answer.

   What does it mean to say that our nation has diversity?

   ○ All of the people are the same.

   ○ There are many differences among people.

   ○ Everyone gets along with each other.

   ○ There are many celebrations.

9. **Explain** what it means to be an ancestor.

   ....

   ....

10. **Describe** one way that Abby from Atlanta, Georgia, celebrates her culture.

    ....

    ....

    ....

11. **Write** one example of a place where you might find diversity in the United States.

    ....

    ....

Go online to write and illustrate your own **myStory Book** using the **myStory Ideas** from this chapter.

THE BIG ? How is culture shared?

The United States is a nation of great diversity. People across the nation celebrate and share their culture in many different ways.

Write three ways that people share their culture with others.

....

....

....

....

....

Draw a picture that shows what you like most about your culture.

While you're online, check out the **myStory Current Events** area where you can create your own book on a topic that's in the news.

Atlas

The United States of America, Political

Washington
★ Olympia

★ Salem

Oregon

Montana
★ Helena

Boise ★
Idaho

North Dakota
★ Bismarck

Mi

South Dakota
Pierre ★

Wyoming

Io
D
★

Carson City ★

Salt Lake City ★

Cheyenne
★

Nebraska

★ Sacramento

Nevada

Utah

Denver ★

Lincoln ★

Sp

California

Colorado

Topeka ★
Kansas

Arizona

Santa Fe
★

Oklahoma

M

Ar

Phoenix
★

New Mexico

Oklahoma ★
City

Litt
Roc

Texas

Lo
E
R

Austin
★

Alaska

Juneau ★

Honolulu
★

Hawaii

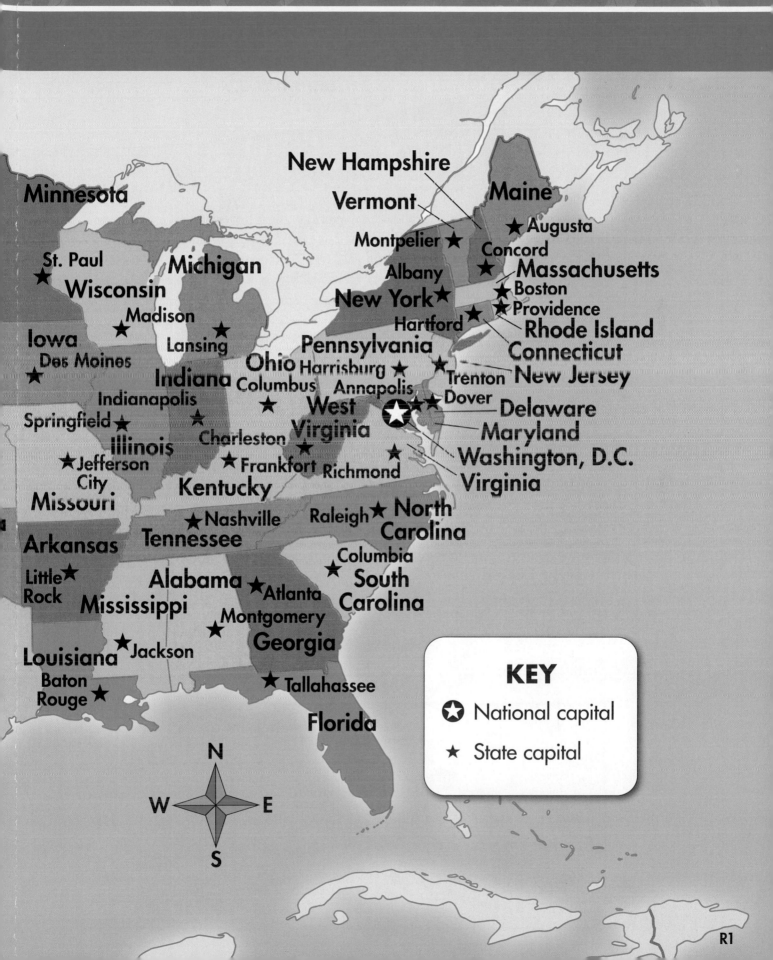

Minnesota

St. Paul ★

Wisconsin

Madison ★

Iowa

Des Moines ★

Michigan

Lansing ★

Illinois

Springfield ★

Indiana

Indianapolis ★

Ohio

Columbus ★

Pennsylvania

Harrisburg ★

New York

Albany ★

New Hampshire

Vermont

Montpelier ★

Maine

★ Augusta

Concord ★

Massachusetts

★ Boston

★ Providence

Rhode Island

Hartford ★

Connecticut

Trenton ★

New Jersey

Dover ★

Delaware

Annapolis ★

Maryland

West Virginia

Charleston ★

Washington, D.C.

Virginia

Richmond ★

Jefferson City ★

Missouri

Kentucky

Frankfort ★

Nashville ★

Tennessee

Raleigh ★

North Carolina

Columbia ★

South Carolina

Arkansas

Little Rock ★

Mississippi

Alabama

★ Atlanta

Montgomery ★

Georgia

Louisiana

Jackson ★

Baton Rouge ★

★ Tallahassee

Florida

N
W   E
S

KEY

★ National capital

★ State capital

R1

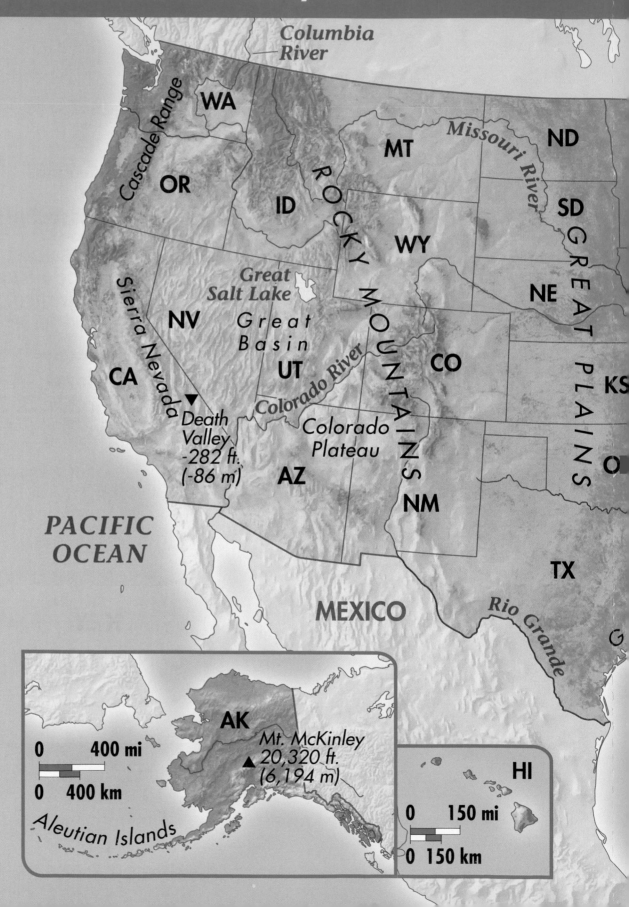

Columbia River

Cascade Range

WA

Missouri River

ND

MT

OR

ID

ROCKY MOUNTAINS

WY

SD

GREAT PLAINS

Great Salt Lake

Great Basin

NV

Sierra Nevada

NE

CA

UT

Colorado River

CO

KS

▼ Death Valley -282 ft. (-86 m)

Colorado Plateau

AZ

NM

PACIFIC OCEAN

TX

MEXICO

Rio Grande

O

0   400 mi

0   400 km

AK

Mt. McKinley ▲ 20,320 ft. (6,194 m)

HI

Aleutian Islands

0   150 mi

0   150 km

CANADA

0   400 mi

0   400 km

Lake Superior

St. Lawrence River

MN

WI

Lake Huron

Lake Ontario

VT

ME

Lake Michigan

MI

NY

NH

MA

IA

IL

IN

OH

Lake Erie

APPALACHIAN MOUNTAINS

PA

CT

RI

NJ

Central Plains

DE
MD

N
W   E
S

KS

MO

Ohio River

WV

VA

Atlantic Coastal Plain

KY

OK

AR

Mississippi River

TN

NC

SC

ATLANTIC
OCEAN

MS

AL

GA

LA

Gulf Coastal Plain

FL

Lake Okeechobee

BAHAMAS

Gulf of Mexico

KEY

— National border
— State border
▲ Highest point
▼ Lowest point

CUBA

The World

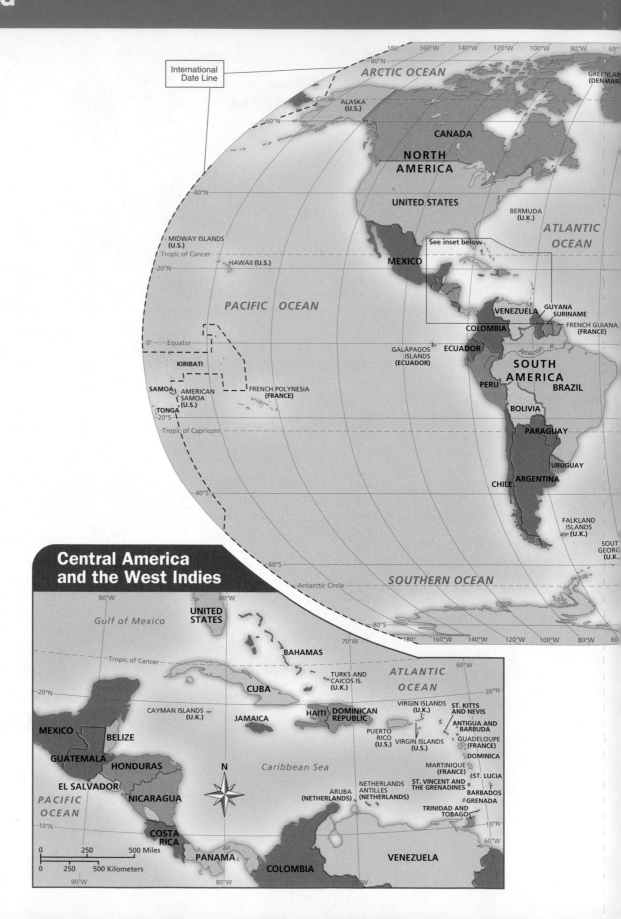

International Date Line

ARCTIC OCEAN

Arctic Circle

GREENLAND (DENMARK)

ALASKA (U.S.)

CANADA

NORTH AMERICA

UNITED STATES

BERMUDA (U.K.)

ATLANTIC OCEAN

MIDWAY ISLANDS (U.S.)

Tropic of Cancer

HAWAII (U.S.)

See inset below

MEXICO

PACIFIC OCEAN

VENEZUELA

GUYANA
SURINAME

FRENCH GUIANA (FRANCE)

COLOMBIA

Equator

GALÁPAGOS ISLANDS (ECUADOR)

ECUADOR

Amazon R.

KIRIBATI

SOUTH AMERICA

PERU

BRAZIL

SAMOA

AMERICAN SAMOA (U.S.)

FRENCH POLYNESIA (FRANCE)

BOLIVIA

TONGA

PARAGUAY

Tropic of Capricorn

URUGUAY

CHILE

ARGENTINA

FALKLAND ISLANDS (U.K.)

SOUTH GEORGIA (U.K.)

SOUTHERN OCEAN

Antarctic Circle

Central America and the West Indies

Gulf of Mexico

UNITED STATES

Tropic of Cancer

BAHAMAS

TURKS AND CAICOS IS. (U.K.)

ATLANTIC OCEAN

CUBA

VIRGIN ISLANDS (U.K.)

ST. KITTS AND NEVIS

CAYMAN ISLANDS (U.K.)

JAMAICA

HAITI

DOMINICAN REPUBLIC

ANTIGUA AND BARBUDA

MEXICO

BELIZE

PUERTO RICO (U.S.)

VIRGIN ISLANDS (U.S.)

GUADELOUPE (FRANCE)

DOMINICA

GUATEMALA

HONDURAS

N

Caribbean Sea

MARTINIQUE (FRANCE)

ST. LUCIA

EL SALVADOR

NICARAGUA

ARUBA (NETHERLANDS)

NETHERLANDS ANTILLES (NETHERLANDS)

ST. VINCENT AND THE GRENADINES

BARBADOS

GRENADA

PACIFIC OCEAN

COSTA RICA

TRINIDAD AND TOBAGO

0   250   500 Miles

0   250   500 Kilometers

PANAMA

COLOMBIA

VENEZUELA

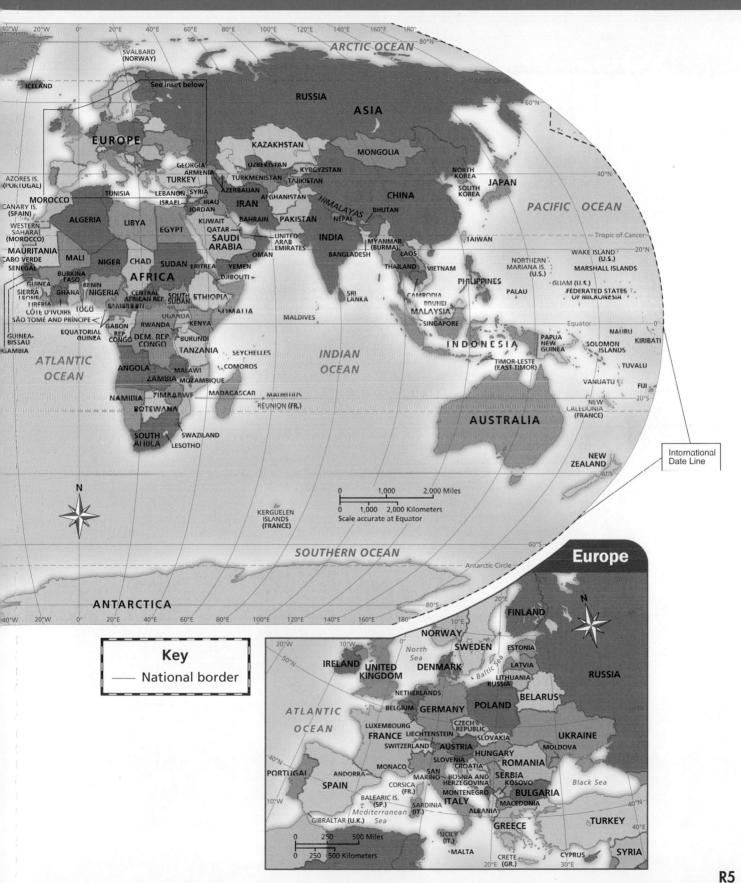

ARCTIC OCEAN

RUSSIA

ASIA

SVALBARD
(NORWAY)

See inset below

ICELAND

EUROPE

KAZAKHSTAN

MONGOLIA

60°N

GEORGIA
ARMENIA
TURKEY

UZBEKISTAN
KYRGYZSTAN

TURKMENISTAN
TAJIKISTAN

NORTH
KOREA

JAPAN

40°N

AZORES IS.
(PORTUGAL)

LEBANON
SYRIA
ISRAEL
IRAQ
JORDAN

AZERBAIJAN

AFGHANISTAN

SOUTH
KOREA

PACIFIC OCEAN

MOROCCO

TUNISIA

IRAN

HIMALAYAS

CHINA

CANARY IS.
(SPAIN)

BAHRAIN

PAKISTAN

NEPAL

BHUTAN

WESTERN
SAHARA
(MOROCCO)

ALGERIA

LIBYA

EGYPT

KUWAIT
QATAR

UNITED
ARAB
EMIRATES

INDIA

MYANMAR
(BURMA)

TAIWAN

Tropic of Cancer

20°N

MAURITANIA

OMAN

BANGLADESH

LAOS

WAKE ISLAND
(U.S.)

CABO VERDE

MALI

NIGER

CHAD

SUDAN

ERITREA

YEMEN

THAILAND

VIETNAM

NORTHERN
MARIANA IS.
(U.S.)

MARSHALL ISLANDS

SENEGAL

AFRICA

DJIBOUTI

GUAM (U.S.)

GUINEA
BURKINA
FASO
BENIN

CENTRAL
AFRICAN REP.

SOUTH
SUDAN

ETHIOPIA

CAMBODIA

PHILIPPINES

PALAU

FEDERATED STATES
OF MICRONESIA

SIERRA
LEONE
LIBERIA
GHANA
TOGO
NIGERIA
CAMEROON

SRI
LANKA

BRUNEI
MALAYSIA

CÔTE D'IVOIRE

UGANDA

KENYA

MALDIVES

SINGAPORE

Equator

NAURU

0°

SÃO TOMÉ AND PRÍNCIPE

GABON
REP.
CONGO

DEM. REP.
CONGO

RWANDA

BURUNDI

INDONESIA

PAPUA
NEW
GUINEA

SOLOMON
ISLANDS

KIRIBATI

GUINEA-
BISSAU
GAMBIA

EQUATORIAL
GUINEA

TANZANIA

SEYCHELLES

INDIAN
OCEAN

TIMOR-LESTE
(EAST TIMOR)

TUVALU

ATLANTIC
OCEAN

ANGOLA

MALAWI

COMOROS

VANUATU

FIJI

ZAMBIA
MOZAMBIQUE

MADAGASCAR

MAURITIUS

NEW
CALEDONIA
(FRANCE)

20°S

NAMIBIA

ZIMBABWE

RÉUNION (FR.)

AUSTRALIA

BOTSWANA

N

SOUTH
AFRICA

SWAZILAND
LESOTHO

International
Date Line

NEW
ZEALAND

40°S

KERGUELEN
ISLANDS
(FRANCE)

0   1,000   2,000 Miles

0   1,000   2,000 Kilometers
Scale accurate at Equator

SOUTHERN OCEAN

60°S

Antarctic Circle

ANTARCTICA

40°W   20°W   0°   20°E   40°E   60°E   80°E   100°E   120°E   140°E   160°E   180°

80°S

Europe

FINLAND

N

NORWAY

SWEDEN

ESTONIA

IRELAND

UNITED
KINGDOM

North
Sea

DENMARK

Baltic Sea

LATVIA

LITHUANIA
RUSSIA

RUSSIA

ATLANTIC
OCEAN

NETHERLANDS

BELGIUM

GERMANY

POLAND

BELARUS

50°N

LUXEMBOURG

FRANCE

LIECHTENSTEIN

CZECH
REPUBLIC

SLOVAKIA

UKRAINE

SWITZERLAND

AUSTRIA

HUNGARY

MOLDOVA

40°N

SLOVENIA
CROATIA

ROMANIA

PORTUGAL

ANDORRA

MONACO

SAN
MARINO

BOSNIA AND
HERZEGOVINA

SERBIA
KOSOVO

Black Sea

SPAIN

CORSICA
(FR.)

MONTENEGRO

BULGARIA

BALEARIC IS.
(SP.)

SARDINIA

ITALY

MACEDONIA

40°N

10°W

GIBRALTAR (U.K.)

Mediterranean
Sea

ALBANIA

GREECE

TURKEY

40°N

0   250   500 Miles

SICILY
(IT.)

MALTA

CRETE
(GR.)

CYPRUS

SYRIA

0   250   500 Kilometers

20°E

30°E

R5

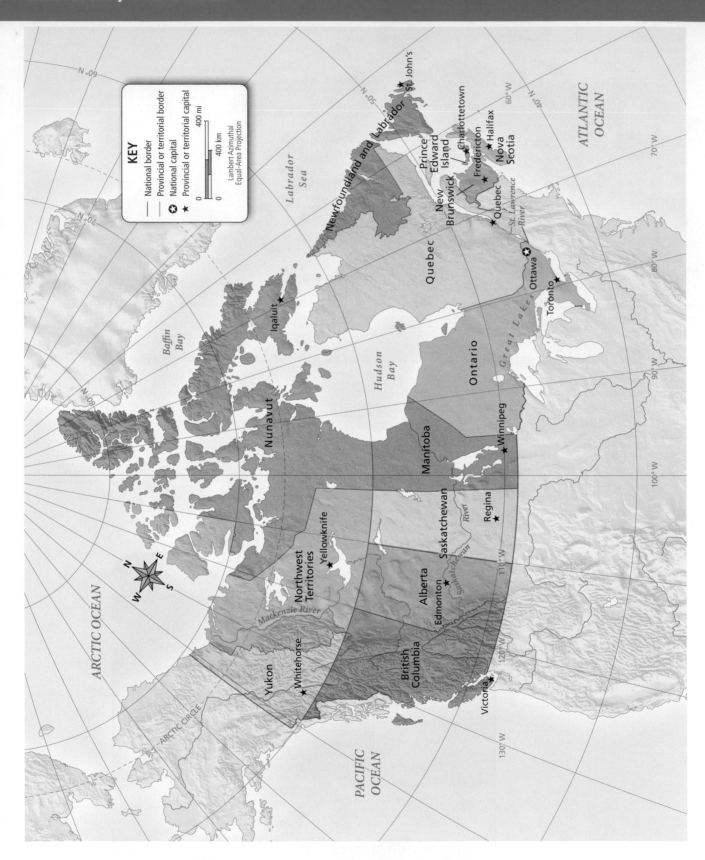

KEY
National border
Provincial or territorial border
National capital
Provincial or territorial capital

400 mi
400 km

Lambert Azimuthal
Equal-Area Projection

ARCTIC OCEAN

PACIFIC OCEAN

ATLANTIC OCEAN

Baffin Bay

Labrador Sea

Hudson Bay

Great Lakes

St. Lawrence River

Mackenzie River

Saskatchewan River

Yukon
Whitehorse

British Columbia
Victoria

Northwest Territories
Yellowknife

Nunavut
Iqaluit

Alberta
Edmonton

Saskatchewan
Regina

Manitoba
Winnipeg

Ontario
Toronto
Ottawa

Quebec
Quebec

Newfoundland and Labrador
St. John's

New Brunswick
Fredericton

Prince Edward Island
Charlottetown

Nova Scotia
Halifax

ARCTIC CIRCLE

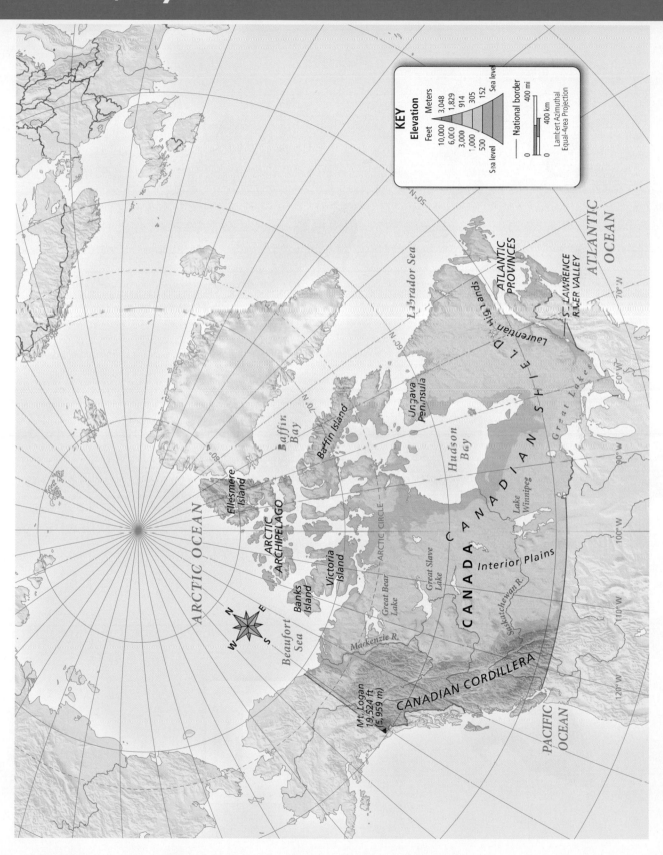

KEY

Elevation

Feet	Meters
10,000	3,048
6,000	1,829
3,000	914
1,000	305
500	152
Sea level	Sea level

—— National border

0   400 mi

0   400 km

Lambert Azimuthal
Equal-Area Projection

ATLANTIC OCEAN

Labrador Sea

ATLANTIC PROVINCES

Laurentian Highlands

ST. LAWRENCE RIVER VALLEY

ATLANTIC OCEAN

Ungava Peninsula

Baffin Bay

Baffin Island

Hudson Bay

Great Lakes

C A N A D I A N   S H I E L D

Lake Winnipeg

Ellesmere Island

ARCTIC ARCHIPELAGO

Victoria Island

Banks Island

ARCTIC CIRCLE

Great Bear Lake

Great Slave Lake

C A N A D A

Interior Plains

Saskatchewan R.

ARCTIC OCEAN

Beaufort Sea

Mackenzie R.

Mt. Logan
19,524 ft
(5,959 m)

CANADIAN CORDILLERA

PACIFIC OCEAN

50°N

60°N

70°N

80°N

70°W

80°W

90°W

100°W

110°W

120°W

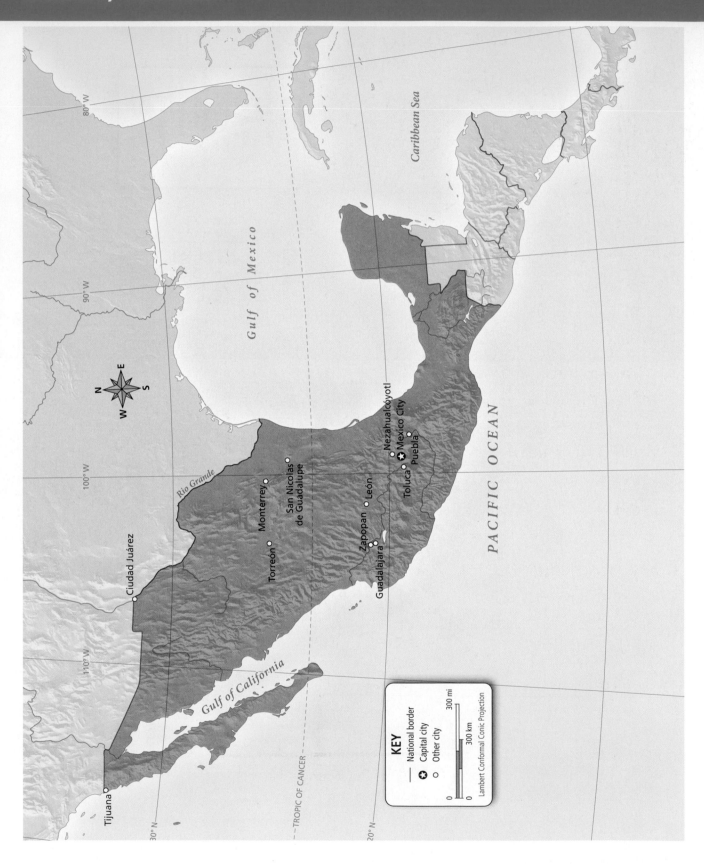

Caribbean Sea

Gulf of Mexico

PACIFIC OCEAN

Gulf of California

Rio Grande

Ciudad Juárez

Tijuana

Monterrey

Torreón

San Nicolás
de Guadalupe

Zapopan

León

Guadalajara

Toluca

Nezahualcóyotl

Mexico City

Puebla

80° W

90° W

100° W

110° W

30° N

20° N

TROPIC OF CANCER

KEY
National border
● Capital city
○ Other city

300 mi

300 km

Lambert Conformal Conic Projection

N E S W

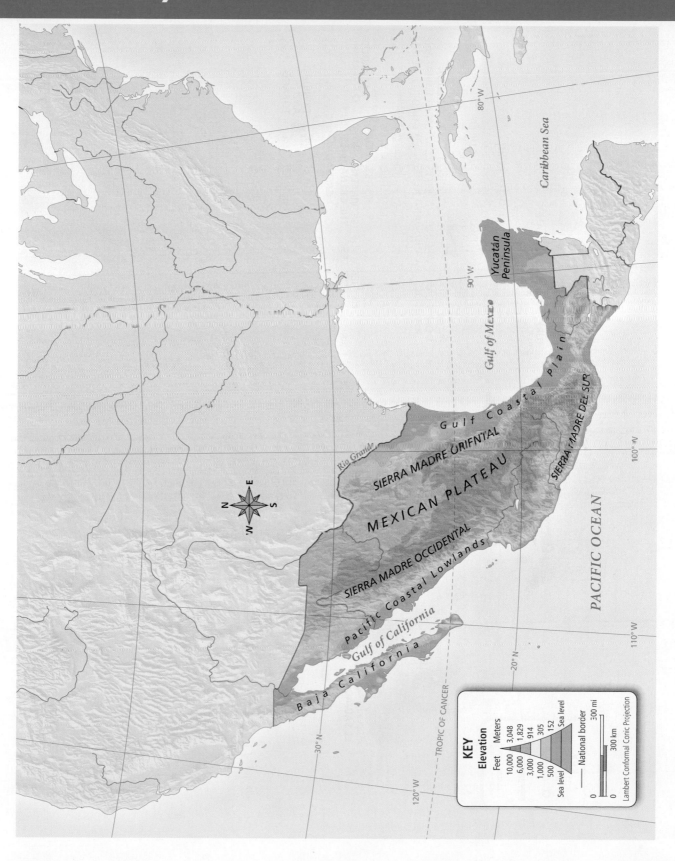

80° W

Caribbean Sea

Yucatán
Peninsula

90° W

Gulf of Mexico

Gulf Coastal Plain

SIERRA MADRE DEL SUR

Rio Grande

SIERRA MADRE ORIENTAL

MEXICAN PLATEAU

N
E
W
S

SIERRA MADRE OCCIDENTAL

100° W

PACIFIC OCEAN

Pacific Coastal Lowlands

Gulf of California

Baja California

110° W

20° N

TROPIC OF CANCER

30° N

120° W

KEY

Elevation

Feet	Meters
10,000	3,048
6,000	1,829
3,000	914
1,000	305
500	152
Sea level	Sea level

—— National border

0   300 mi

0   300 km

Lambert Conformal Conic Projection

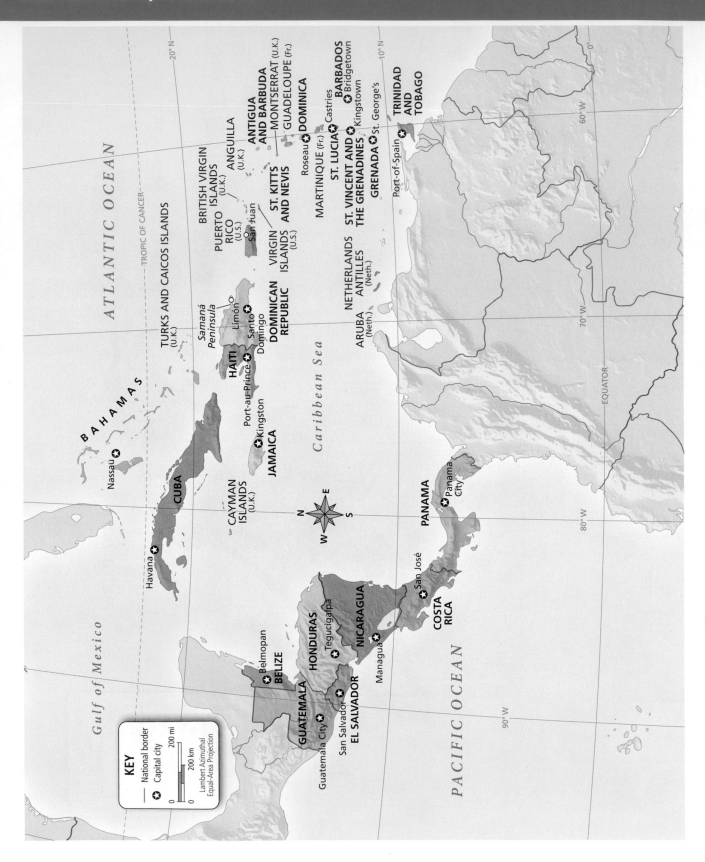

ATLANTIC OCEAN

20° N

10° N

TROPIC OF CANCER

ANTIGUA
AND BARBUDA
MONTSERRAT (U.K.)
GUADELOUPE (Fr.)

ANGUILLA
(U.K.)

BARBADOS
Bridgetown

DOMINICA

Roseau

BRITISH VIRGIN
ISLANDS
(U.K.)

ST. KITTS
AND NEVIS

MARTINIQUE (Fr.)

ST. LUCIA Castries

TRINIDAD
AND
TOBAGO

PUERTO
RICO
(U.S.)
San Juan

VIRGIN
ISLANDS
(U.S.)

ST. VINCENT AND
THE GRENADINES Kingstown

GRENADA St. George's

Port-of-Spain

TURKS AND CAICOS ISLANDS
(U.K.)

NETHERLANDS
ANTILLES
(Neth.)

60° W

Samaná
Peninsula
Limón

ARUBA
(Neth.)

70° W

Santo
Domingo

DOMINICAN
REPUBLIC

HAITI

Port-au-Prince

Caribbean Sea

EQUATOR

BAHAMAS

Kingston

Nassau

JAMAICA

CUBA

CAYMAN
ISLANDS
(U.K.)

E

N   S

W

PANAMA

Panama
City

80° W

Havana

Gulf of Mexico

San José

NICARAGUA

COSTA
RICA

HONDURAS

Tegucigalpa

Belmopan

BELIZE

Managua

PACIFIC OCEAN

GUATEMALA

Guatemala City

San Salvador
EL SALVADOR

90° W

KEY

— National border

✪ Capital city

0   200 mi

0   200 km

Lambert Azimuthal
Equal-Area Projection

Glossary

A

absolute location (ab′sə lo͞ot′ lō kā′shən) Where exactly a place is located on Earth.

abundance (ə bun′dəns) A lot of something.

activist (ak′tə vist′) Someone who works to make a change happen.

adapt (ə dapt′) To change the way you do something.

adobe (ə dō′bē) Sun-dried bricks used to build shelters and other buildings.

agricultural region (ag′ri kul′chər əl rē′jən) A place where there is much flat land and rich soil.

amendment (ə mend′mənt) A change to a constitution.

ancestor (an′ses′tər) A relative who lived long ago.

anthem (an′thəm) A song of loyalty to a nation.

arts (ärts) Paintings, sculptures, songs, stories, and dances.

assembly line (ə sem′blē līn) Each worker does only one part of a job.

B

bank (bank) A business that keeps, exchanges, and lends money to people.

barter (bärt′ər) To give a good or a service to another in exchange for a different good or service.

bill (bil) An idea for a law that is written down for the government to decide on.

boycott (boi′kät′) When people refuse to do something for a reason.

budget (buj′it) A plan that shows a person's income, expenses, and savings.

C

Cabinet (cab′ə nit) A group of advisors, or people who tell a leader, such as the U.S. president, what they think about a subject.

canal (kə nal′) A waterway that is dug by people.

capital resource (kap′ət ′l rē ′sôrs′) Something that is needed to produce goods and services.

cardinal direction (kärd′′n əl də rek′shən) North, south, east, or west.

cause (kôz) Something that people feel strongly about.

census (sen′səs) A count of the population.

citizen (sit′ə zən) An official member of a community.

civil rights (siv′əl rīts) Rights of all citizens to be treated equally under the law.

climate (klī′mət) The weather that a place has over a long period.

Pronunciation Key

a in hat	ō in open	′l in cattle
ā in age	ô in order	′n in sudden
ä in father	o͞o in tool	th in weather
e in let	u in cup	zh in measure
ē in equal	ᵾ in reverse	
i in it	ə a in ago	
ī in ice	e in agent	
o in hot	o in collect	
	u in focus	

colonize (käl′ən īz′) To settle lands for another country.

colony (käl′ə nē) A place ruled by another country.

communicate (kə myo͞o′nə kāt) To pass thoughts or information to others.

community (kə myo͞o′nə tē) A place where people live, work, and have fun together.

confederacy (kən fed′ər ə sē) A formal agreement or treaty between groups to work together.

Congress (kän′grəs) The legislative branch of United States government.

conserve (kən surv′) To save and protect something.

constitution (kän′stə to͞o′shən) A written plan of government that explains the beliefs and laws of a state or nation.

consumer (kən so͞om′ər) A person who spends money to buy things he or she needs or wants.

continent (känt′′n ənt) One of the seven largest land areas on Earth: Asia, Africa, North America, South America, Antarctica, Europe, and Australia.

convention (kən ven′shən) A large meeting.

cooperate (kō äp′ər āt′) To work together.

council (koun′səl) A group that makes laws.

credit (kred′it) A promise to pay for something.

credit card (kred′it kärd) A card used in place of money that lets the cardholder buy things and pay for them later.

cultural region (kul′chər əl rē′jən) An area where people who share a similar culture live.

culture (kul′chər) The way of life of a group of people.

custom (kus′təm) A special way of doing something that is part of a person's culture.

debt (det) Money that is owed to another person.

deed (dēd) An action.

delegate (del′ə git) A person chosen to act for others.

demand (di mand′) The amount of goods or services that people want and can buy.

democracy (di mäk′rə sē) A form of government in which people vote to choose who leads the community, state, or nation.

deposit (dō päz′it) The money a person puts in a bank.

diverse (də vurs′) Different.

diversity (də vur′sə tē) When there are many differences among people.

division of labor (də vizh′ən əv lā′bər) When a project is divided, or broken down, into smaller jobs.

drought (drout) A period of time when there is not enough water.

ecosystem (ē′kō sis′təm) An area where all living things, such as the plants and animals, interact with each other.

elevation (el/ə vā/shən) The height of land above sea level.

equal rights (ē/kwəl rīts) When all people have the same rights.

erosion (ē rō/zhən) The washing away of soil by rain, wind, and nearby rivers.

exclusion (eks klōō/zhən) Keeping people out of a place.

executive (eg zek/yōō tiv) Describes the branch of government that enforces, or carries out, the laws.

expedition (eks pə dish /ən) A trip made for a special reason.

explorer (ek splôr/ər) A person who travels looking for new lands and discoveries.

export (ek spôrt/) To send products and resources from one country to another country.

folk tale (fōk tāl) A fictional, or made-up, story that is passed down by tradition.

fort (fôrt) A strong building or area that can be defended against enemy attacks.

free market (frē mär/kit) People can choose what to make and what to buy.

frontier (frun tir/) A region that forms the edge of a settled area.

gold rush (gōld rush) A time period in the late 1840s when thousands of people came from around the world to California to search for gold.

goods (goods) Things that people make or grow and then sell.

government (guv/ərn mənt) A system of ruling people.

governor (guv/ə nər) The head of a state's executive branch who is elected by the people in a state.

harvest (här/vist) The crops gathered at the end of the growing season.

hemisphere (hem/i sfir) A part into which Earth is divided by lines of latitude and longitude.

hero (hir/ō) A person who is a role model for others.

homestead (hōm/sted/) An area of land that includes a house and its buildings.

human resource (hyōō/mən rē/ sôrs/) A person who makes products or provides services.

immigrant (im/ə grənt) A person who moves from one country to settle in a different country.

import (im pôrt/) To bring products and resources into one country from another.

independence (in/dē pen/dəns) Freedom.

industrial region (in/dus/trē əl rē/jən) A place where many kinds of factories are located.

interdependence (in/tər dē pen/dəns) When people depend on each other to get the things they need and want.

interest (in'trist) The money a bank gives a person for letting it hold his or her money.

intermediate direction (in'tər mē'dē it də rek'shən) Northeast, southeast, northwest, or southwest.

interpreter (in tur'prə tər) A person who helps people who speak different languages understand each other.

invention (in ven'shən) Something that is made for the first time.

irrigate (ir'ə gāt') To bring water in through pipes.

judicial (jōō dish'əl) Describes the branch of government that makes sure laws are fair.

landform (land'fôrm') The form or shape of part of Earth's surface.

landmark (land'märk') A building or other structure that is important to a culture.

legend (lej'ənd) A story from the past whose facts cannot be checked.

legislative (lej'is lāt tiv') Describes the branch of government that makes laws.

legislature (lej'is lā'chər) A part of government that makes laws.

liberty (lib'ər tē) Freedom.

loan (lōn) The money a bank lends to people.

location (lō kā'shən) A place where something is.

longhouse (lông'hous') A Native American home that is longer than it is wide.

mayor (mā'ər) A leader of a community.

mine (mīn) To dig for materials.

mineral (min'ər əl) A resource that does not come from an animal or a plant.

mission (mish'ən) A settlement that has a church where religion is taught.

modify (mäd'ə fī') To change something, such as the physical environment.

motto (mät'ō) A saying.

natural resource (nach'ər əl rē'sôrs') Something found in nature that is useful to people.

needs (nēdz) Things you must have to live.

nonrenewable resource (nän ri nōō'ə bəl rē'sôrs') A natural resource that takes a long time to replace or cannot be replaced after it is used.

opportunity cost (äp ər tōō'nə tē kôst) The value of the thing you give up when you choose one thing over another.

oral history (ôr'əl his'tə rē) A story that is only spoken.

P

patent (pat′′nt) A document that gives a person the right to be the only one making or selling an invention.

patriot (pā′trē ət) A person who loves and defends his or her country and upholds people's rights.

pilgrim (pil′grəm) A person who travels for a religious reason.

pow wow (pou′wou′) A Native American gathering.

producer (prə dōōs′ər) A person who makes a product or provides a service.

profit (präf′it) The money that businesses have left after their costs are paid.

protest (prō test′) To complain.

Q

Quaker (kwā′kər) A follower of a religion that believes in peace and equal treatment for all people.

R

recreation (rek′rē ā′shən) A way of enjoying oneself.

recycle (rē sī′kəl) To use an item again.

region (rē′jən) An area with common features that set it apart from other places.

relative location (rel′ə tiv lō kā′shən) A description of where a place is in relation to other places.

renewable resource (ri nōō′ə bəl rē′sôrs′) A natural resource that can be replaced in a short time.

represent (rep′ri zent′) To speak for others.

representative (rep′rə zen′tə tiv) A person chosen to speak for others.

reservation (rez′ər vā′shən) Land that the United States government set aside for Native Americans many years ago.

revolution (rev′ə lōō′shən) When people want to take over the government that rules them and create a new one.

route (rōōt) The course you take to get somewhere.

rural (roor′əl) Describes a community in the countryside where there is plenty of open space.

S

savings (sā′vings) The money a person earns but does not spend.

scarcity (sker′sə tē) When there is not enough of something to meet people's needs and wants.

segregate (seg′rə gāt′) To separate.

service (sur′vis) Work that one person does for another.

specialization (spesh′əl ə zā′shən) When each person in a group has a special skill and does one job or one part of a project.

strike (strīk) When workers stop working until things change.

suburban (sə bur′bən) Describes a community near a large city.

suffrage (səf′rij) The right to vote.

supply (sə plī′) The amount of goods or services that people can sell.

symbol (sim′bəl) On a map, a small picture or shape that stands for a specific location, settlement, or building. In a work of art, a picture that stands for an idea.

tax (taks) Money paid to a government.

technology (tek näl′ə jē) The scientific knowledge about how things work.

telegraph (tel′ə graf′) A machine that sends and receives signals through a thin wire.

territory (ter′ə tôr′ē) An area of land owned by a country either within or outside the country's borders.

toll (tōl) Money that is paid for using a road.

trade (trād) To use money to buy and sell goods and services.

tradition (trə dish′ən) A special way that a group does something that is part of its culture.

transcontinental (trans′kän tə nent′l) Across the continent.

union (yōōn′yən) A group of workers that joins together.

urban (ur′bən) Describes a community in a large city.

vaccine (vak sēn′) A shot with a weak virus that helps people's bodies fight off disease.

value (val′yōō) What an item is worth to a person.

vegetation (vej′ə tā′shən) Plant life.

veto (vē′tō) To reject.

volunteer (väl ən tir′) A person who improves the community and helps others.

wagon train (wag′ən trān) A group of covered wagons that travels together for safety.

wants (wänts) Things you would like to have but do not need.

weather (weth′ər) The daily conditions outside.

Index

This index lists the pages on which topics appear in this book. Page numbers before an *m* refer to maps. Page numbers before a *p* refer to photographs. Page numbers before a *c* refer to charts or graphs. Page numbers before a *t* refer to timelines. **Bold** page numbers indicate vocabulary definitions.

Credits

Text Acknowledgments

Grateful acknowledgement is made to the following for copyrighted material:

Page 267 "Introduction to Our Second Catalog of Native American Literature" by Joseph Bruchac from *http://lopezbooks.com/articles/bruchac/*. Copyright © 1996 by Joseph Bruchac.

Note: Every effort has been made to locate the copyright owners of the material produced in this component. Omissions brought to our attention will be corrected in subsequent editions.

Illustrations

CVR1, 24 Lyn Boyer; **CVR2, 127, 128, 129** Angus Cameron; **1, 2, 3, 4, 5, 6, 7, 8** Mike Lester; **3, 208** Siffert; **22** Paul Eric Roca; **43, 44, 45** Christine Larsen; **55, 74, 166, 167, 249** Mattia Cerato; **91, 107, 196, 265, 266, 267** Tin Salamunic; **100, 190** Rick Whipple; **144** Laura Huliska-Beith; **176** Dave Kirwin; **187, 188, 189** Dan Masso; **204, 205** Marsha Grey Carrington; **206, 250** Robin Storesund; **242** Agnes Yi; **278** Kory Heinzen.

Maps

XNR Productions, Inc.

Photographs

Every effort has been made to secure permission and provide appropriate credit for photographic material. The publisher deeply regrets any omission and pledges to correct errors called to its attention in subsequent editions.

Unless otherwise acknowledged, all photographs are the property of Pearson Education, Inc.

Photo locators denoted as follows: Top (T), Center (C), Bottom (B), Left (L), Right (R), Background (Bkgd).

Cover

CVR1 (CL) Jeff Greenberg/PhotoEdit, Inc., (CR) Jon Spaull/©DK Images, (BL) moodboard/Alamy, (C) NASA, (CL) Rob Atkins/Getty Images, (T) SuperStock; **CVR2** (B) Konstantin L/Shutterstock, (TR) North Wind/North Wind Picture Archives, (CC) Sami Sarkis Lifestyles/Alamy, (BL) North Wind Pictures Archive/Alamy

Frontmatter

v (BR) Look Photography/Corbis; **vi** (BL) Brian Cook/Alamy; **vii** (BR) North Wind Picture Archives/©Associated Press; **viii** (BL) Jon Spaull/©DK Images; **ix** (BR) JLP/Jose L. Pelaez/Corbis; **x** (BL) Mary Evans Picture Library/Alamy Images; **xii** (BL) Peter M. Fredin/©Associated Press.

Text

12 George Doyle/Stockbyte/Thinkstock; **14** Thinkstock; **15** Jupiterimages/Thinkstock; **16** (BL) Bruce Leighty/Ticket/PhotoLibrary Group, Inc., (TR) Fackler Non CC/Alamy Images; **17** (TL) Ohio Historical Society; **18** (TR) Grafton Marshall Smith/Corbis, (BL) steffstarr/Fotolia; **19** (TR) Jim West/Alamy Images; **20** (BR) Bobby Deal/RealDealPhoto, 2010/Shutterstock, (BL) Library of Congress; **23** (TR) BMD Images/Alamy Images; **27** (TR) ©DK Images; **28** (TR) Juice Images/Alamy; **32** (T) Chad Ehlers/Alamy Images, (T) dbimages/ Alamy Images, (B) Stephen Saks Photography/Alamy Images; **33** (TR) ©DK Images, (TR) Look Photography/Corbis; **34** (TR) Glowimages/Getty Images, (R) Photodisc/White/PhotoLibrary Group, Inc.; **35** (B) Hemera/Thinkstock; **36** (TR) Liane Cary/age fotostock/PhotoLibrary Group, Inc.; **38** (TL) Jason Hosking/Corbis; **42** (Bkgrd) Alaska Stock LLC/Alamy Images; **46** (TL) Antoine Beyeler, 2010/Shutterstock, (BL) NASA/Corbis, (CL) PETER HARRISON/PhotoLibrary Group, Inc.; **48** (CR, BR) Mike Norton, 2010/Shutterstock; **49** (BC) Benn Mitchell/Getty Images, (TR) John Elk III/Alamy Images, (TL) Nagel Photography/Shutterstock; **50** (TR) Caitlin Mirra, 2010/Shutterstock, (CR) Jeff Banke, 2010/Shutterstock; **51** (TR) Patrick Eden/Alamy Images; **52** (L) ©Martin Harvey/Corbis, (TR) Stephan von Mikusch/Fotolia (TC) Peter Kirillov, 2010/Shutterstock; **54** (BR) Global Warming Images/Alamy Images; **56** (TR) Brian Cook/Alamy, (CR) Papilio/Alamy Images; **60** (TR) Galyna Andrushko/Shutterstock, (CL) Lonely Planet Images/Alamy Images; **62** (TR) Hemera/Thinkstock; **63** (TR) moodboard/Alamy; **64** (TR) ©Morgan Lane Photography/Shutterstock, (BR) Commercial Eye/Getty Images; **66** (CR) Lazar Mihai-Bogdan/Shutterstock; **68** (TR) Chad Ehlers/Alamy Images, (CL) Danita Delimont/Alamy Images; **69** (CR) Yvette Cardozo/Alamy Images; **70** (R) Andy Z./Shutterstock; **71** (R) Ivan Bondarenko/Shutterstock; **72** (R) Disney Channel/Getty Images; **73** (TR) Daniel Grill/Tetra Images/Corbis; **82** (TR) Charlotte Observer/McClatchy-Tribune/Getty Images; **83** (CR) CLM/Shutterstock, (CR) spiritofamerica/Fotolia; **84** (TR, BR) ©The Granger Collection, NY; **85** (TC) North Wind/North Wind Picture Archives; **86** (CR) Stephen J. Boitano/©Associated Press; **88** (R) Stephen J. Boitano/©Associated Press; **89** (CR) Burstein Collection/Corbis; **90** (TR) ©Ilja Masik/Shutterstock; **92** (B) North Wind Pictures Archive/Alamy; **94** (B) PoodlesRock/Corbis; **98** (TR) The Granger Collection, NY; **99** (TL) Witold Skrypczak/Getty